Rodo Santoro

Palermo and Monreale

Arnone Editore - Palermo

Offices and Administration: Via Francesco Crispi 120 - 90139 Palermo (Italy) – Tel./Fax 0916 124 007
Depot: Via Filippo Patti 25 - 90133 Palermo - Tel. 091 333 461 - Fax 091 333 484
http://www.arnoneeditore.com • Email: info@arnoneeditore.com

Text: Rodo Santoro
Photographs: Carmelo Sammarco

Photographs on pages 14, 16 bottom, 17, 18, 20, 27 bottom, 45, 49, 84, 114 bottom, 115, 116 top, 126, 127, 128, 129 by Paolo Arnone
Photographs on pages 1/2, 19, 22/23, 30 bottom, 97 bottom, 100, 101, 102, 113 top,114 bottom, 116 bottom, 117 top, 120, 124, 125 bottom by Lanfranco Angeli
Photographs on pages 73, 92, 103, 104, 107, 108, 109 by Publifoto
Photographs on pages 21, 117 bottom, 118/119, 121, 122, 123, 125 top by Enzo Lo Verso
Photographs on pages 8, 21, 37, 54, 55, 75, 78 top right, 80, 86, 99 top, 105, 106 middle and bottom from the Arnone Editore *archives*

Layout, graphics, cover and image research: Saverio Rao
Translation: Quid Traduzioni e Servizi Linguistici - Palermo (Claudia Ricchiari)
Image digitization: Litoscanner - Palermo
Printed and bound by: Officine Grafiche Riunite - Palermo

ISBN 88-87663-22-X

FOREWORD

Framed by the glorious scenery of the mountains overlooking the Conca d'Oro, the Mount Pellegrino promontory and the Tyrrhenian Sea, Palermo is one of the most ancient cities of the Mediterranean and, with its monuments, one of the most beautiful cities in Italy. Its surroundings – coasts, mountains and plains – are still covered with the luxuriant and varied Mediterranean vegetation: from lemon trees to agave plants, from prickly pears to olive trees, from maritime pines to aromatic plants and flowers; the climate is almost evenly temperate throughout the year, except on summer days when the sirocco wind blows.

The earliest settlers were Sicans, Sicels, Cypriots, Carthaginians and Greeks, who formed the basis of the original ethnic group. Later, the long-lasting Roman and Byzantine (Constantinople's) rule constituted an important historical, political and cultural continuum which shaped and amalgamated the local populations, introducing Graeco-Latin culture and Christianity. Palermo (the ancient *Panormos*) was one of the Italian cities where Roman civil institutions proved more enduring, from 254 BC to 831 AD, including the period of Byzantine administration (the Roman Empire reunited by Constantinople). Then the bloody Saracen invasion ravaged Sicily for more than a century, from 827 to 965, with continuous local wars and massacres. This was the island's most tragic period, which ended in 1072 with the liberation of Palermo by the army of Robert "the Guiscard" and Roger of Hauteville. With the creation of the Kingdom of Sicily by the Hautevilles, Palermo finally reached the height of its splendour, which lasted from 1130 to the end of the 13C. Then, while maintaining its prerogatives as a royal seat, the city passed under the rule of the Chiaramontes, one of the most powerful aristocratic families of the island. In 1414, with the unification of the Crowns of Sicily and Aragon, the long-lasting period of the viceroys began. This, however, did not affect Palermo's magnificence: in the 17C and 18C the city even witnessed a second period of splendour, marked by the flourishing of architecture and arts in general. Between the 18C and 19C it became one of the "musts" of the so-called *Grand Tour* which men of culture from all countries used to make round the main Italian cities. Among these famous visitors were Goethe, Brydone, Houel, Hugo, etc. Originally a commercial emporium, but later transformed into the seat of the government and aristocracy, between the 19C and the early 20C Palermo became an elegant middle-class city which, unfortunately, was damaged by the air bombings of 1943 and by the intense building activity of the 1950s-60s.

Today, the tourist visiting Palermo and its environs can discover, even during a short stay, the immense architectural mosaic of its past, from the Graeco-Punic ruins to the early-medieval cathedral, from the 14C feudal castle to the sumptuous baroque churches, down to the elegant forms of *liberty* architecture (Italian *Art Nouveau*), a style which had in Palermo one of its world capitals. This outstanding artistic and cultural heritage is strewn throughout a territory characterized by remarkable natural beauties: it stretches down to the sea but also comprises a mountainous hinterland, rich in woods and natural attractions. Between the mountains and the sea are small but pleasant and luxuriant plains, the most famous of which is the Conca d'Oro, with its typical vegetation mostly consisting of citrus orchards, especially lemon trees.

The main centres of the Province are Termini Imerese, Piana degli Albanesi, Partinico, Monreale, Bagheria, Carini, Terrasini and Caccamo, each with a rich historical heritage and folklore of its own. Palermo can be easily reached thanks to a system of national and international connections. Its airport is linked to the main national and European cities, and there are regular ferry services to and from Genoa, Naples, Tunis and Sardinia. The Palermo-Catania, Catania-Messina and Palermo-Messina motorways (the last of which is nearing completion) directly link the city to the national

motorway system. In short, in this area nature and history combine to offer a most interesting stay. The great artistic heritage and the temperate climate, which have always been admired and appreciated, have made Palermo and its environs an attractive destination for tourists and visitors also during the past centuries. This ancient tradition has resulted in the development of a wide range of accommodation facilities.

* * *

And now a few words about the layout of this guide. The city's history and monuments are presented in chronological order. The text has thus been divided into chapters, each focussing on a homogeneous phase of Palermo's history. Hence, a single chapter may deal with one or more centuries. Each chapter has a short historical introduction, followed by descriptions of the monuments. At the end of some of these is a concise discussion of one particular aspect of the history, art, or social and cultural life of the city. For instance: the city walls and gates; the markets; historical villas and gardens; museums; the great festivals. Of course, historical architecture, archaeology and art in general are given the lion's share in a guide like this. The selection of monuments and sites has been based on criteria such as their historical and artistic importance, and their accessibility.

Royal eagle on the façade of the Royal Palace.

Palermo's peculiar history has also made necessary the adoption of a few guidelines which the reader should be aware of, concerning the numeration of the kings of Sicily and the different names of some buildings and works of art. It should be borne in mind that, in some cases, the name of a Sicilian sovereign may follow different numeration criteria. This may be due to various reasons. For instance, a sovereign may, at the same time, have been an emperor, as it was the case for Frederick Hohenstaufen: he was Frederick I of the Crown of Sicily, and II of the Empire. However, it should be noticed that, according to the numeration of the Crown of Sicily, the true Frederick II is Frederick of Aragon. There are also cases of triple numeration: King Ferdinand of Bourbon, Charles of Bourbon's son, was Ferdinand III of Sicily, IV of Naples and I of the Kingdom of the Two Sicilies, as a consequence of the political vicissitudes of his reign. In order to avoid continuous and lengthy explanations, the numeration of the *Regnum Siciliae* has been preferred here.

As for monuments bearing different names, the reason is that in Palermo these are often better known by a characteristic "historical" name. In such cases, however, the reader will find all the names of the building or work of art indicated in the title of the relevant section.

* * *

Along the coast, in the immediate vicinity of Palermo, are a number of bathing establishments and beaches. The best-equipped bathing resort is undoubtedly Mondello, but you can also find small coves and beaches near the characteristic old fishing villages, which offer you the chance to bathe in the Tyrrhenian Sea (Capo Gallo, Sferracavallo, Terrasini, Porticello, Solanto, Trabia, etc.). Long beaches stretch both eastwards and westwards, but these take us beyond the city's environs.

It is not possible to illustrate with photographs all the places, monuments and objects of art mentioned in the text. There is such a great number of historical buildings, works of art, archaeological sites and natural beauties that the result would have been a cumbersome volume. In laying out this guide, special emphasis has thus been placed on the great monuments which require more images for a thorough description. For other monuments and works of art, a single photograph of identification has been provided, while others are simply described in the text.

THE ORIGINS

The caves of Mount Pellegrino

Mount Pellegrino. Engravings in the "Addaura 2" cave, detail.

The entire area of Mount Pellegrino is rich in archaeological evidence. However, only the famous wall engravings in the Addaura Caves will be described here, at the beginning of this guide. These caves are to be found on the northern slope of the mountain, looking onto the sea, and are easy to reach. They are of natural origin and were inhabited at different historical ages. Some of them are particularly vast. The so-called "Addaura Caprara" cave, for instance, is more than 2 km deep. The wall engravings in the so-called "*Addaura 2*" cave (90 m above sea level) were discovered in 1952 by Jole Bovio Marconi. They have been dated between the end of the Upper Paleolithic and the beginning of the Mesolithic. One of them, depicting the main scene, has become famous among scientists at international level because of its peculiar features. Experts have recognized four different though not very distant phases of execution of the engravings. The scene is characterized by deeply-cut lines and by the presence of numerous human figures, dynamically represented in an extremely realistic style, as are the different animals depicted (horses, deer, cattle). But what does the famous scene represent? Various explanations have been given by different experts. According to some, the scene depicts a ritual dance for the initiation to puberty of some youths. The characters have masks, shaped like a bird's head with a long beak, and bushy hair. The two central figures are moving acrobatically. According to a different interpretation, the two central figures have been tied up for sacrifice, while the others are dancing around them in a propitiatory rite. In a third version, the two central figures are victims of the dreadful practice known as "incaprettamento" (in which someone's arms, legs and neck are bound together so that they choke to death; from "capretto", calf, because it recalls the way calves are tied up for transportation). According to a fourth and final interpretation, the scene depicts a ritual game in which the two central characters are "thrown" from one surrounding character to another.

Slope of Mount Pellegrino looking down onto Palermo.

The Punic necropolis

The Punic necropolis is situated within the "Tuköry" barracks. The first tombs were accidentally discovered in 1867; later, in 1928, the archaeologist P. Marconi carried out the first survey of the area (chamber tombs preceded by a stepped *dromos*). Only in 1989 did the Superintendence of the Cultural and Environmental Heritage of Palermo carry out the first excavation campaign. Recently, the necropolis has been given a systematic organization which makes the site well worth a visit. The area re-arranged by the Superintendence is about 1000 sq m large. The excavated tombs, rich in archaeological remains, belong to different Punic tomb types. Most of them are chamber tombs, dug entirely in the calcarenite bank which characterizes the area. They consist of a rectangular funeral chamber preceded by a stepped access. The entrance was closed by large slabs and marked by a sepulchral pillar. The chamber contains a monolithic sarcophagus, covered with slabs or tiles. The tomb furnishings range from the 6C to the 4C BC, when the old necropolis was filled in and replaced by a new necropolis characterized by terracotta cinerary urns buried in holes. All the finds are displayed at Palermo Archaeological Museum.

Tomb in the Punic necropolis.

The Porta d'Ossuna catacombs

This is the largest remaining catacomb complex of the early Christian age in Palermo, which can be entered from Corso Alberto Amedeo no.110. The network of tunnels, with burial niches and arcosolia, is dug in tufa. These subterranean galleries are presumed to have originally been quarries for the extraction of tufa, which was shaped into blocks and used for building in Punic-Roman Panormos. Later, the early Christians used them as a burial site, as they also did with the other underground quarries of the ancient city, such as those under the Jesuit Church of Casa Professa.

THE CAPITAL OF A COSMOPOLITAN KINGDOM (the 13th century)

The name of the city is of Greek origin, as it derives from the word *Panormos*, meaning "all harbour" but also translated by some as "many harbours". In fact, it was the spacious and easily accessible port (of which only the present-day *Cala* remains) that favoured the earliest settlements and the founding of the city on a hill bounded to the north by the depression of the Papireto River (so called because of its lush papyrus vegetation) and to the south by the Kemonia (both rivers now flow underground). Between the mouths of the two rivers lay the ancient port, a deep bay with an irregular outline which, in the course of the centuries, gradually silted up and was reduced to the present-day Cala. The area has been inhabited since prehistoric times, as is witnessed by the wall engravings found in the caves of Mount Pellegrino and ascribed to the Upper Paleolithic. Reliable historical evidence indicates the presence of the Sicans in the 12C BC, followed by the Cypriots, Cretans, Elymi and Greeks. The first permanent urban settlement, however, was founded by the Phoenicians between the 8C and the 7C BC. The *Paleapolis* (from the Greek "old city") lay on the upper part of the oblong rocky spur bounded by the two rivers (in the area now occupied by the Royal Palace, Piazza Vittoria and the Archbishop's Palace, as far as Via Roma) and was surrounded by strong city walls. A second city, the *Neapolis* (from the Greek "new city"), was later built between the two rivers, but outside the city walls, in a lower position and closer to the port.

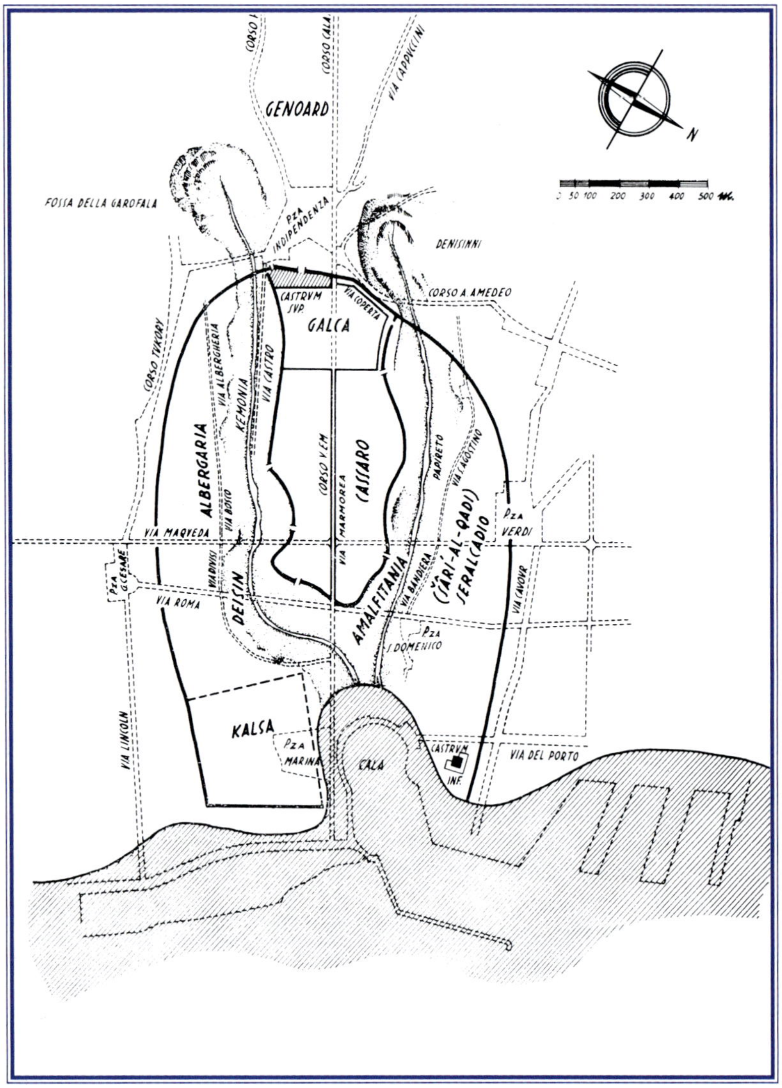

Plan of the development of Palermo from the 6C to the 14C (as reconstructed by R. La Duca).

From 485 BC to 306 BC Panormos was involved in the long struggle for supremacy between the Greeks and Carthaginians, with alternating alliances, battles and long truces (Battle of Himera: 480 BC). In 272 BC the city opened its gates to Pyrrhus, king of Epirus and a great commander, who proclaimed himself king of the Sicilians, though with no practical consequences. From 254 BC Panormos was under Roman rule. Traces of this period can be found in some architectural remains in the present-day tropical garden of Piazza Vittoria (better known as Villa Bonanno). Here a mosaic floor depicting wild boar and lion hunting can still be seen. The floors of another two constructions are displayed at Palermo Archaeological Museum. Christianity soon flourished and spread in the city, as is still witnessed by the presence of a series of catacombs, including the famous ones of the Papireto (Porta d'Ossuna).

In 536, the Gothic garrison which had occupied the city was driven out by general Belisarius, and Palermo passed under the rule of Byzantium (Constantinople), which had reunited the Roman Empire. During the following long-lasting period of peace numerous churches were built: Santa Maria della Pinta (erected by Belisarius); the

Church of the Madonna Odigitria (also known as "d'Itria", or of Constantinople, the patron saint of Sicily) and the Church of the Benedictines. But, most importantly, the Cathedral was built between 590 and 604 on the initiative of Bishop Victor. Two Palermitans, Agatho and Sergius, became Roman Popes and were later canonized. In 732, the Byzantine emperor Leo the Isaurian decreed that Palermo's diocese should pass under the ecclesiastical jurisdiction of the Patriarchate of Constantinople. From 827 to 965 Sicily was under the bloody rule of the Saracens. Palermo was stormed by the Saracens in 831, after a one-year heroic resistance. During their occupation, the upper part of the city was called *Casr* (from the Latin *Castrum*, later *Cassar-Cassaro*) and became the first seat of the governor. In 937 another government citadel was built near the port, the *Hal-Halisah* (later Kalsa). The Muslims turned Palermo's churches into mosques. The same fate befell the ancient Cathedral, dedicated to the Virgin Mary, which became the so-called "Friday mosque".

King Roger II crowned by Christ. Mosaic dating from the first half of the 12C, in the Church of the Martorana, Palermo. The iconographic model is that of the coronation ceremonies of the Byzantine emperors in Constantinople of the same period.

In 1072 the city was liberated by a Christian army led by Roger I, Great Count of Sicily, and Robert "the Guiscard", of the Hauteville family, who had been mandated by the Pope in Rome. Palermo thus began to regain its splendour and, within a few years, it was to become the political and economic centre of the Mediterranean. In 1130, in fact, it became the capital of the Kingdom of Sicily, and on Christmas Day that same year the first king, Roger II of Hauteville, was crowned in the Cathedral, which was restored to the Christian cult. Trade and cultural activities had already recovered and were thriving again, favoured by Palermo's position as the capital of a great kingdom which stretched from Montecassino to Albania and the North African coasts of Tunisia and Libya. Byzantine art and culture flourished again, combining with the architectural tradition of the Maghreb and the Latin cultural influences from central Italy and northern Europe. Roger II added architectural splendour to the *Castrum Superius*, which became his Royal Palace. Inside this complex construction, in 1132, he built his Palace chapel (the "Palatine Chapel"), dedicated to St Peter, which is the most magnificent example of medieval art in Palermo. Meanwhile, the city was enriched with splendid buildings and new boundary walls. The Churches of San Giovanni dei Lebbrosi, San Giovanni degli Eremiti, San Cataldo, Santa Maria dell'Ammiraglio (the "Martorana") were all built in this period. Just outside the city walls, Roger II created a large park with woods, plantations, stock farms, artificial lakes and luxury royal residences: Maredolce, Favara, Parco (Altofonte), Minnermo.

Roger II was succeeded by William I, who built the Zisa royal residence (*Domus in Solatium*) within the great royal park which lay between Palermo and the surrounding mountains. William I was followed by William II, who built the Cuba. During

The Kamelaukion *(calotte crown) of the Sicilian sovereigns, in the Cathedral Treasury.*

his reign the Hauteville dynasty reached the height of international prestige. In his attempt to reaffirm the prerogatives of the "apostolic legateship" which, by papal concession, enabled the kings of Sicily to appoint bishops, the king met with opposition from the archiepiscopal curia of Palermo. As a consequence, he promoted the construction, within the boundaries of the Royal Park, of the great Duomo of Monreale and of the nearby Benedictine monastery and Royal Palace. This immense church is another gem of medieval architecture in Sicily. The interior is richly decorated with splendid Byzantine mosaics and the cloister is one of the highest and most elegant expressions of medieval sculpture applied to architecture. In the meantime, from 1170 to 1184, the old Palermo Cathedral was partially demolished and reconstructed as a much larger building on the initiative of Bishop Gualtiero, who transformed it into the greatest cathedral of medieval Sicily.

Palermo's sovereigns, though vassals of the Popes in Rome, often tended to pursue an autonomous international policy aimed at conquering the Eastern Empire, whose political ideology, ceremonials and clothes they imitated. This was one of the reasons why men of science and letters, politicians and artists from all over the world gathered at Palermo's court, turning it into a magnificent centre of international culture. Among the most famous international statesmen who were active at the Palace, shaping the Kingdom's policy, were George of Antioch and Maio of Bari, who first raised the question of the unity of Italian peoples in the Middle Ages. The Royal Palace also housed the royal art and crafts workshops, where crowns, jewels, precious furnishings and ceremonial clothes were made. Some of these can still be admired today, such as the splendid *Kamelaukion*, a Byzantine imperial crown now displayed in the Cathedral Treasury.

The Royal Palace ("Palazzo dei Normanni") and Palatine Chapel (San Pietro)

Palermo's Royal Palace is the most famous historical palace in the city and one of the most important in Italy. It was the seat of the kings and viceroys of the Kingdom of Sicily, and now houses the Sicilian Regional Assembly. In 1984, during renovation work in the "Duke of Montalto's Rooms", an imposing architectural structure was brought to light which represented an exceptional archaeological discovery pertaining to the ancient city walls. The ruins date from three historical phases. The first (5C BC) is a stretch of the west walls, with a large gate flanked by two towers and a postern defended by a turret. The second section (4C-3C BC) is very close to the first and has an opening corresponding to the gate. The third and more external stretch of walls has no opening (the gate had been blocked up) and probably dates from the 13C, when Roger II built his Royal Palace. The history of the site prior to the construction of the

Royal Palace.
East front looking onto the old town.

Palace is still controversial. It was presumably occupied by a building used by the Byzantine and, later, Saracen governors. The Royal Palace was probably begun around 1130, the year of the coronation of Roger II of Hauteville as first king of Sicily. Medieval chronicles define the building *Palatium Novum* or *Castrum Superius*, to distinguish it from the *Palatium Vetus* or Castellammare. In 1132, work began on the Palatine Chapel, dedicated to St Peter; its mosaic decoration was continued under Roger's successors, William I and William II. The royal apartments (of which some rooms remain today) were also completed, as well as all the other architectural structures such as the Pisana Tower with the Throne Room, the Greca Tower, the Chirimbi, etc.

Frederick II lived in the Royal Palace mostly during his youth. The building began to lose its importance towards the end of the 13C, and particularly through the 14C,

Royal Palace, King Roger's Rooms. Right: Facing peacocks (12C mosaic). Below: A room.

so much so that, in 1392, the royal seat was moved to the Chiaramontes' *Steri* palace, confiscated from the members of this family following their rebellion against the Crown. In the 15C and the early 16C, the ancient Royal Palace, deserted and totally neglected, gradually fell into decay. From 1513 to 1553 it was the seat of the Inquisition, which shared it with a small garrison. Meanwhile, in 1536, the royal architect Antonio Ferramolino had ordered the demolition of the higher parts of the towers (which had become easy targets for siege batteries) and the construction of bulwarks in a more forward position, with a view to strengthening the Palace's defences.

In 1553, after adequate renovation work, the Palace became the residence of the viceroys, while the Inquisition moved out. For some seventy years, the viceroys ordered substantial architectural and decorative work. In 1560 the great bastion (still extant) overlooking Piazza Indipendenza was built, as was the structure linking the Pisana and Greca Towers (the latter was also renovated). In 1569-71 the magnificent construction which was to house the Great Hall of the Sicilian Parliament was built. The upper Courtyard, known as the Fountain Courtyard, and the loggia of the Hall of Parliament were added in 1571-72. In 1599, the great Maqueda (or Lower) Courtyard was laid out. In 1678-82, the portraits of the former viceroys were placed in the Grand Gallery.

Other extensions were added on the occasion of Charles of Bourbon's coronation in Palermo. The Red, Yellow and Green Rooms were built in 1787. In 1791, King Ferdinand of Bourbon had an Observatory built on the Pisana Tower. From this Observatory, in 1801, Giuseppe Piazzi discovered the asteroid which was named Cerere Ferdinandea (Ceres) after the king. Other works and new furnishings were added during the two stays of King Ferdinand between the end of the 18C and the beginning of the 19C. In this period (1811-12), the painter Giuseppe Velasco decorated the ancient Hall of Parliament with frescoes depicting the Labours of Hercules; hence the new name given to the hall where the Sicilian Regional Assembly now meets: the Hall of Hercules. Unfortunately, during the struggles for autonomy of 1820 and 1848 the Royal Palace was assailed and sacked. Repairs and refurbishment were made possible by the Bourbon restoration of 1850. After 1860 the building passed to the House of Savoy, and in 1922 it was partly assigned to the Ministry of Education. After the concession of regional autonomy to Sicily (1946), the building became the seat of the Regional Assembly.

Royal Palace, Maqueda Courtyard.

* * *

The long entrance hall leads to the main courtyard, which features a portico and a double order of loggias. The staircase on the left leads up to the first floor, where a great loggia leads into King Roger's splendid Chapel, known as the "Palatine Chapel" (dedicated to St Peter), built in 1132 and inaugurated in 1140. Before entering the Chapel, you can admire a small portico with lancet arches, Egyptian granite columns and, on the internal walls, 19C mosaics which have replaced the originals. The church is in the Sicilian "mixed" plan, with a nave and two aisles divided by rows of columns bearing arches. The nave is covered by a magnificent stalactite wooden ceiling. The raised Byzantine Sanctuary has three apses. The central square area, enclosed with mosaic screens, is covered by a hemispheric dome resting on angular niches. At the beginning of the nave is the great marble royal throne. Near the presbytery, on the right, is a precious ambo resting on columns and an imposing Paschal candlestick, 4.5 m

high, decorated with plant motifs and inlaid figures (12C). Impressive mosaics on a gilded background almost uniformly decorate the upper walls of the Chapel. The work of Byzantine artists and local craftsmen, they were executed in 1143 (presbytery and apse) and in the following twenty years (nave). The cupola features the figure of Christ Pantocrator giving his blessing, surrounded by angels and archangels; in the drum are the four Prophets: David, Solomon, Zacharias and St John the Baptist; eight busts of saints adorn the pendentives. On the arches of the presbytery is the Annunciation and the Presentation to the Temple; in the bowl-shaped vault of the central apse is the figure of the blessing Christ, while the underside of the arch depicts the throne of Judge-

Opposite page: Royal Palace, Palatine Chapel.
Top: External loggia.
Bottom: Central apse.

Royal Palace, Palatine Chapel.
Top: Transept wing.
Bottom: The cupola depicting Christ Pantocrator.

ment. On the right side of the Chapel are scenes from the life of Christ: the Nativity, Baptism and Transfiguration, Lazarus' Resurrection, the Entry into Jerusalem; on the left side is the Madonna Odigitria with figures of saints. The nave is decorated with later mosaics depicting scenes from the Old Testament, while

Royal Palace, Palatine Chapel. Mosaics depicting the Nativity and the Entry of Christ into Jerusalem.

Opposite page: Royal Palace, Palatine Chapel. The pulpit and the Paschal candlestick in sculpted marble.

Royal Palace, Palatine Chapel. Christ Pantocrator in the bowl-shaped vault of the central apse.

the aisles portray stories of St Paul and St Peter. At the opposite end of the nave, above the royal throne, is a 14C mosaic depicting Christ enthroned between St Peter and St Paul.

An imposing staircase leads to the upper floor, where the former royal apartments can be visited. In the Pisana Tower is a large central room (perhaps the ancient Throne Room), 15 m high, square in plan and covered by cross vaulting; underneath is the Treasury Room. The so-called Roger's Room (actually built at a later date) is entirely

Palatine Chapel Treasury. Ivory and golden bronze casket (Fatimid Egyptian art, 12C).

decorated with splendid mosaics depicting an enchanted garden with plants and exotic animals (perhaps the Royal Park). The series of rooms is completed by the Room of the Winds and the King's Guard's Room. The Hall of Hercules (where the Sicilian Regional Assembly meets) is particularly interesting, with its neoclassical frescoes by the painter Giuseppe Velasco, depicting the labours and apotheosis of Hercules. The Viceroys' Room is also worth visiting: it owes its name to the collection of portraits of viceroys and lieutenants of Sicily it contains. Past the apartments is the astronomic Observatory (not open to the public) on the Pisana Tower, founded in 1786. From this observatory the astronomist Giuseppe Piazzi, the director, discovered the asteroid Ceres in 1801. It now houses an astronomical laboratory of the University of Palermo.

Palermo Cathedral (Maria Santissima Assunta)

The present-day building is the outcome of a superimposition of additions and alterations carried out in various periods from the 12C onwards. Of the original Cathedral, however, nothing seems to have remained, and very little information has come down to us. We know that the old Cathedral – called the Basilica of Santa Maria – was founded in 592 by Bishop Victor, on the orders of Pope Gregory the Great, and consecrated in 604 by Bishop John. It was presumably square in plan, and smaller than the present-day building. After the Saracen conquest of the city, the church was turned into the "Friday mosque", all the images were abolished and the furnishings dispersed, and this is how it must have appeared when the Hauteville brothers, Robert "the Guiscard" and Roger, conquered the city in the 11C. The rather decayed building was restored to the Christian cult, but was seriously damaged by earthquakes, particularly that of 1169. The church was in a state of such disrepair that, in the same year, Bishop Gualtiero ordered that it should be demolished and reconstructed as a more majestic building. Work began between 1170 and 1172: the great Sanctuary was built (with the three apses facing east and the exterior decorated with stone inlays), as were the long architectural body of the nave and aisles and the four stairway towers at the corners of the building. But the construction remained unfinished. It seems, in fact, that the original project included a segmental dome resting on a polygonal drum. Work on another building, the Duomo of Monreale, was carried out in the same period, though with a substantial difference: while Palermo Cathedral was financed by the scanty resources of the Archiepiscopal Curia, the Duomo of Monreale was financed by the Royal Treasury.

The Cathedral – almost completed in 1185 – was dedicated to Our Lady of the Assumption and staged the sumptuous

Cathedral. South front looking onto the square. Its parts date from various periods (12C-19C).

Cathedral. South triple-arched portico, a masterpiece of Palermo's 15C architectural syncretism.

Cathedral. The nave after the renovation work of 1781-1801.

coronations of the Hauteville and Hohenstaufen sovereigns. Their royal tombs were placed in the interior. Work was resumed twice during the 13C (1220; 1260), when the stairway towers were completed. It was continued in the 14C, with the decoration of the west front (1352-53). The elegant south entrance portal (1426) was executed by Antonio Gambara and later enriched with the sumptuous triple-arched portico facing the Cathedral Square (1453). The wooden door with carved figures was the work of Francesco Miranda de Castellammare (1432). In the 15C, numerous chapels were added to the sides of the aisles. The famous marble Retablo by Gagini, a scenographic sculptural ensemble which decorated the central apse and its corner walls, was executed in the 16C. In the same period, six windows of the nave were walled up. Another sixteen were walled up in 1652.

At the end of the 18C, a number of works were carried out which almost completely transformed the original medieval aspect that the church had maintained until then. The "renovation" of the Cathedral was entrusted to the architect Ferdinando Fuga, and work was begun in 1781 and finished in 1801. In the interior, the Gaginesque Retablo was dismantled. The groups of four columns each, bearing the pointed arches of the aisles, were incorporated into pillars which now supported a continuous horizontal entablature. The wooden trusses of the roof were replaced by barrel-vaulting. Other alterations were carried out in the Sanctuary, which was surmounted by a large dome supported by a tall drum. The overall result was a rather hybrid exterior, while the interior took on the gelid aesthetic forms of Classicism. To top it all, in 1826-35 the architect E. Palazzotto erected a bizarre neo-medieval construction, serving as a belfry, on the high tower facing the west front (perhaps a stronghold of the Punic-Roman city walls). The ancient Cathedral built by Bishop Gualtiero has come down to us with all these changes, alterations and additions.

Cathedral. Tomb of King Roger II of Hauteville. The porphyry sarcophagus is still the temporary tomb built in the 12C.

* * *

The Cathedral is now entered through the magnificent south portico, after crossing a quadrangular square surrounded by a marble balustrade with statues of saints and Palermitan bishops placed at regular intervals (Piano della Cattedrale, i.e. Cathedral Square). The south portico consists of three large pointed archways and is one of the most elegant porticoes of the Sicilian 15C. The Portal has fine wooden doors with figures skilfully carved by Francesco Miranda de Castellammare. The interior of the church contrasts sharply with the exterior. Its present aspect is the result of extensive alterations carried out between 1781 and 1801, based on a project by the architect Ferdinando Fuga of Florence. He renovated the church interior in a mixed style which combined baroque and neoclassical forms, also adding the great dome which definitively altered the external medieval aspect of the Cathedral. Some of the chapels of the north flank house the large silver urns containing the relics of three of the four patron saints of Palermo: St Rosalia, St Christine and St Ninfa. The monumental urns are the work of famous 17C Palermitan silversmiths. St Rosalia's urn is carried in proces-

sion on 15 July, during the *Festino* (feast) of the *Santuzza*, as Palermitans affectionately call their main patron saint. The Crypt is a suggestive medieval space, lying beneath the great apses and protruding beyond them. It is covered by barrel vaults and houses 23 sarcophagi (some of which Roman and reused) containing the relics of Palermo's Archbishops.

The royal tombs are placed in the enclosed chapels to the left of the south entrance. There are six tombs, four surmounted by stone canopies and two set into the walls. They contain the relics of some of the most famous sovereigns of the Kingdom of Sicily and their wives: Roger II, Henry VI, Constance of Hauteville, Frederick Hohenstaufen. Those set into the walls are the sarcophagi of Constance II of Aragon and William of Athens, the son of Frederick II (of the Aragonese of Sicily). The present arrangement of the tombs dates back to the end of the 18C, when they were moved here from their original place to the left of the choir. The most interesting, from a historical and artistic point of view, are the two red porphyry sarcophagi (those of Frederick and his father, Henry VI). These monumental tombs were actually ordered by Roger II in the 12C, and the choice of the hard Egyptian red porphyry – an imperial prerogative – reveals the political ambitions of the first sovereign of Sicily. The tombs had remained in the Duomo of Cefalù for a few decades, then they were moved to Palermo Cathedral where, in the 13C, Frederick earmarked them for himself and his mother. From the point of view of their form, with the lower portion resembling the keel of a boat, they are not comparable to any other type of western medieval royal sarcophagi, and the extremely skilful execution accounts for their outstanding artistic and historical value.

Cathedral. The porphyry sarcophagus of Frederick II also contains the remains of two other historical personages. Built in the 12C for King Roger II, the sarcophagus remained empty for a long time, until it was chosen by Frederick II as his own tomb.

The Cathedral Treasury contains the splendid crown found in Constance of Aragon's sarcophagus and known as "Queen Constance's Crown". In fact, it is a genuine Byzantine imperial *Kamelaukion*. In addition to this extremely precious calotte crown, which (once again) bears witness to the imperial ambitions of the Sicilian sovereigns, the Treasury displays vestments of exquisite craftsmanship and altar-frontals, including a pallium interwoven with pearls and decorated, in the centre, with a gold bas-relief depicting a small Madonna, a gift by Archbishop Carandolet.

Two tall and large pointed arches link the Cathedral to the complex of the Archbishop's Palace, overlooking Via Matteo Bonello. Next to the west front of the Cathedral is the Chapel of the Coronation (Cappella dell'Incoronata) where, according to some historians, the coronation of Roger II took place in 1130, due to the precarious conditions of the old Cathedral prior to the restructuring work ordered by Bishop Gualtiero.

Church of Santa Maria dell'Ammiraglio (or "Martorana"), now San Nicola di Mira

Church of Santa Maria dell'Ammiraglio (Martorana). Bell tower and mosaic of the Nativity.

Built on an embankment flanking Via Maqueda and Piazza Bellini, this is Palermo's Greek Orthodox cathedral. The building, now generally known as the Martorana, is actually the medieval Church of Santa Maria dell'Ammiraglio. It owes its popular name of "Martorana" to Eloisa Martorana, who in 1193 founded a Benedictine convent to which King Alfonso "the Magnanimous" annexed the church in 1453. The construction is characterized by a combination of deutero-Byzantine and baroque architectural elements. Built around 1143 as a private church by George of Antioch, Grand Admiral to King Roger II, in the 19C it was restored to its original medieval beauty by the architect Patricolo. The building was originally conceived as a central-plan church, with a square structure covered by a dome supported by a polygonal drum resting on four columns – hence, a typical Byzantine church of the middle period, corresponding to the Comnenus imperial dynasty of Constantinople. In the 15C, it was annexed to the contiguous Benedictine convent. From 1588 onwards it underwent major alterations. The west front was demolished, the portico and narthex were removed and the church was linked to the bell tower by a "Latin" nave which considerably lengthened its plan.

The interior was decorated with a continuous cycle of mosaics, which have only partly maintained their original aspect. Among those which can still be admired today are Jesus and Four Angels, in the cupola; the Annunciation, in the triumphal arch; the four Evangelists, in the vault; the Nativity of Christ and the Dormition of the Virgin. In the lateral apses are the figures of St Joachim and St Anne. These finely executed mosaics date from the first half of the 12C, thus from an earlier age than those in the Palatine Chapel. The 17C-18C paintings are the work of several Sicilian and foreign painters, including Antonino Grano, G.

Salerno known as "lo Zoppo di Gangi", Wilhelm Borremans, Olivo Sozzi and Vincenzo da Pavia. The church, which still observes the Byzantine rite followed by the Sicilian communities of Greek-Albanian origin, contains some valuable Byzantine icons, including one dedicated to St Nicholas. The four-storey bell tower was built later than the original church, and is partly similar to the stairway towers at the four corners of the Cathedral. The small columns of the upper storeys "lighten" the architectural mass with their peculiar arrangement. At present, the church is the sister Cathedral of the Byzantine Eparchy of Piana degli Albanesi.

Church of Santa Maria dell'Ammiraglio (Martorana). Central apse.

Church of San Cataldo

The Church of San Cataldo, facing Santa Maria dell'Ammiraglio, was built around 1154 by Maio of Bari, Grand Admiral and Grand Chancellor to King William I, as a private chapel. The charming interior is typical of medieval Sicilian constructions. Rectangular in plan, it is completely unadorned; its austerity harmonizes with the exterior, covered by three small and characteristic cupolas which follow the longitudinal axis of the building. This type of structure is reminiscent of the Apulian churches with three longitudinally-oriented cupolas. It may thus be argued that Maio of Bari ordered a similar-style church as his own private chapel in Palermo. The cupolas, however, are typically Palermitan in style – i.e. hemispherical calottes resting on a tall cylindrical drum provided with windows, so as to admit light into the church. It should be pointed out that the red colour of the cupolas is the result of modern alterations. The church is now presided over by the Knights of Malta, and can be visited in the presence of the keeper.

Top: Church of San Cataldo.

Bottom: Church of San Giovanni dei Lebbrosi.

Church of San Giovanni dei Lebbrosi

According to the historian Fazello, this was the first monument built by the monks who arrived in Palermo with the Christian army that freed the city in 1072. In fact, it was presumably built on the orders of Robert "the Guiscard" and Roger while they were besieging the city occupied by the Saracens. It owes its name to the leper hospital which was adjoined to the church shortly after its construction. The interior has a nave and two aisles, covered by a wooden roof. The bell tower is a 20C reproduction of the original. The overall structure of the building anticipates the distinctive features of Palermo's medieval churches, i.e. the combination of part of the centrally-planned Byzantine church covered by a dome and with three projecting apses, with the nave and aisles of the Latin basilicas, which went to form the Sicilian "mixed" plan.

Church of San Giovanni degli Eremiti. Bottom: The Cloister.

Church of San Giovanni degli Eremiti

This is a composite architectural complex which consists of the remains of a church built before the year 1000, then transformed into a Muslim mosque and later restored to the Christian cult, a cloister (the only vestiges of a Benedictine monastery) and a church built around 1142. These elements are unified by the vegetation of a pleasant and luxuriant garden, which gives the complex an enchanting atmosphere. The partially rebuilt bell tower and the church are decorated by five "bare" cupolas; the interior is cross-shaped and unadorned, as in the Church of San Cataldo. It should be pointed out that the aspect of the cupolas was altered by a brilliant red colour, arbitrarily added during the work carried out in the 20C. The complex, as we see it today, reflects the restoration work supervised by the architect Patricolo in 1882. The openings were originally covered with open-work plaster sheets; those visible today are 19C copies of an original kept in Palermo Archaeological Museum.

Church of the "Magione" (Santissima Trinità)

Probably built around 1150 by the Royal Protonotary and Chancellor Matteo d'Aiello, the church was originally entrusted to the Cistercian monks. For a period it then belonged to the Teutonic Knights, and went through various vicissitudes until 1787, when it passed under the direct control of the Bourbon monarchy. The church is one of the most austere medieval monuments still extant today. While retaining its severe forms, it has undergone a process of architectural refinement resulting from the continuous cultural development of the stoneworkers. The interior is divided into a nave and aisles, and covered by wooden roofs (reconstructed after the air bombings of the last war). The floor is scattered with tombstones of Teutonic Knights. The church, in fact, was entrusted to this religious order of knighthood by Emperor Henry VI Hohenstaufen, for the specific purpose of providing spiritual and material assistance to the German pilgrims who happened to pass through Palermo. Renovation work carried out in modern times has restored the essential medieval structures to their original purity, eliminating later (mainly neoclassical) additions. Some of the later stylistic additions, however, can still be seen in the interior, such as a stucco by Vincenzo Gagini, depicting the Pietà, in the first chapel on the right. The left apse has a small Renaissance portal. Adjoining the church is the cloister, with the traditional motif of intertwined arches.

Church of the Magione (Santissima Trinità). Entrance front. Bottom: Central apse and transept.

Church of Santo Spirito (or "del Vespro")

The church is located within the cemetery of Sant'Orsola, at the end of Via dei Vespri. Together with the Cistercian monastery, it was built by Bishop Gualtiero during the reign of William II. It was here that the Palermitan uprising against the Angevins (Sicilian Vespers) broke out on Easter Monday 1282, after a young Sicilian woman was insulted by a Spanish soldier. After various alterations carried out in the 15C and 16C,

Church of Santo Spirito. The Revolution of the Sicilian Vespers (1282) broke out in front of this church.

the church was abandoned until 1782, when Viceroy Caracciolo decreed that a burial ground should be created in the area. The ancient monastery and the original cloister were demolished. At the end of the last century, the church was restored to its original form. Of the medieval building, the apses and the two lateral fronts with geometric lava stone decorations remain, while the main front has been destroyed. The interior reflects the Sicilian mixed plan of Palermo and Monreale Cathedrals, though on a smaller scale. It is divided into a nave and two smaller aisles, separated by eight ogival arches resting on pillars. The sanctuary is on a higher level than the nave and aisles. Behind the high altar is a 15C crucifix on shaped wood.

The Zisa

During his reign, Roger II created a Royal Park which, in medieval times, occupied the territory now bounded by the Royal Palace, Maredolce, Parco and Monreale. This consisted of a large woodland area which was at the same time a game reserve (where monarchs and princes would go hawking) and a garden dotted with buildings and artificial lakes, exotic plants and other amenities. Numerous royal buildings and residences were erected within its boundaries – the *Domus* – also called *Solatia* (from the Latin *Solatium* = psychological and moral compensation for the toil of everyday life) from the name given to the royal estates.

Zisa (a Domus*). Façade.*

The most famous among the *Solatia* of the ancient Royal Park was built by William I between 1165 and 1180, and curiously owes its name (Zisa) to a Persian-Arabic word used to designate the king: *Al Aziz*, i.e. "the Glorious one". The building is now being restored after a long period of neglect. Although popularly known as a "castle", it is actually a palace (a *Domus*). More than any other monument erected by the Sicilian monarchs, its elevation clearly reflects the prism-shaped model of the Donjon (or early-medieval embattled tower), although

Zisa. Coat of arms on the façade.

Zisa. Mosaic of the royal eagle of Sicily.

Zisa. The Iwan room with its small fountain.

reinterpreted as a pleasure residence. It is rectangular in plan, and two storeys high. Single- and two-light windows and two lateral turrets "lighten" the mass of the building which, having lost the fortified aspect of the medieval embattled towers, became one of the earliest examples of aristocratic palace in Europe. Outside, a small lake enhanced the pleasant atmosphere of the place. A number of building and decorative features, and above all the presence of two spaces – the *Iwan* and the Hall of the Winds, typically found in North Africa influenced by Fatimid Egyptian architecture – indicate that the builders of the Zisa must have been craftsmen of Fatimid culture from the Maghreb, particularly from the territories of Ifriquia ruled by the Crown of Sicily. The *Iwan* (or *Diwan*) – the room with three exedrae on the ground floor – is an architectural feature of remote Hittite-Persian origin which was in fashion for centuries. In the *Iwan* of the Zisa, a fountain set against the wall supplied water to a small artificial stream which served to cool the room. Above the *Iwan*, on the first floor, was the Hall of the Winds, a roofless terrace surrounded by a portico resting on four angular columns which, due to its characteristic layout, was pleasantly ventilated.

The Cuba (Cuba Sottana)

This is one of the *Solatia* of the ancient Royal Park, built by King William II in 1180 (thus later than the Zisa). The Palace is architecturally similar to the Zisa. Here again, the structure is based on a combination of elements: the Donjon, *Iwan* and Hall of the Winds. The prism-shaped construction is very high, and was formerly surrounded by an ar-

Top: Cuba, internal courtyard. Stucco muqarna *(cell-like niche, stalactite work). Bottom: Cuba (*a Domus*).*

tificial lake. On the upper edge of the building, a Cufic inscription records the year of construction (1180) and the king who ordered it (William II). In spite of its height, the building consists of only three rooms: a vestibule at the entrance; a large Hall of the Winds in the centre; the *Iwan* at the far end. The Palace is thought to have been the residence of the royal mistresses, on account of the fact that it only had one small access, that its high walls were pierced by small windows but only from some height upwards, and that it was surrounded by an artificial lake. A novel in Boccaccio's *Decameron*, in fact, describes the Cuba as the place which between the 13C and 14C was still the residence of the most beautiful girls offered to the king of Sicily.

The small Cubula pavilion, near Villa Napoli.

The Cubula

Not far from the Cuba, within the Villa Napoli estate (the old Cuba Soprana or Alfaina Tower), is the Cubula, which can be entered from Corso Calatafimi no. 575. This is a small and graceful 12C construction, quadrangular in shape and covered by a typically Palermitan "bare" cupola. It has an ogival archway on each side, and was probably a kind of pavilion situated at the edge of a fishpond.

FROM THE MIDDLE AGES TO THE 16th CENTURY

After the death of William II, in 1189, the Crown of Sicily passed from the Hauteville dynasty to the Hohenstaufens. The short and tragic reign of Henry VI was followed by a return to ancient splendour in 1208, with the accession to the throne of Henry's son, Frederick (I of Sicily; II of the Empire). He was a great statesman, well-versed in administration, natural science and mathematics, but rarely stayed in Palermo with his court. On his death (1250), a period of political unrest began which certainly did not benefit the city. Palermo thus started to slowly lose its role of predominance in the Mediterranean, while Naples was gradually increasing its prestige. The Crown of Sicily (a vassal of the Holy See) was assigned by the Pope to Charles of Anjou, the brother of the king of France. The Angevins went so far as to subject Sicily to military occupation and this led to the Revolution of the Sicilian Vespers, which broke out in Palermo on Easter Monday 1282, leading to the expulsion of the Angevins from the island. The legitimate heir to the throne was King Peter of Aragon who, supported by the Sicilian nobility, was crowned king of Sicily in Palermo on 4 September 1282. Unlike the 12C, the 13C in Palermo was not characterized by the construction of great architectural works. However, two outstanding churches were begun in the second half of the century: Sant'Agostino and San Francesco.

Frederick II on his throne with a hawk, from his work "De arte venandi cum avibus"*. The sovereign stayed at his court in Palermo mostly during his youth.*

With the only exception of Frederick II of Sicily, the Aragonese dynasty of Sicily, which had replaced the Angevins, proved to be weak. In the 14C, in fact, the great aristocratic families gained effective control of the island thanks to their economic and military power. The most important – the Alagona, Peralta, Ventimiglia and Chiaramonte families – as a matter of fact divided Sicily into four spheres of influence. This was thus known as the period of the four Vicars; Palermo was under the rule of the powerful Chiaramonte family. But, in 1392 – after about a century of political weakness on the part of the Crown of Sicily, and after the dubious outcome of the lengthy War of the Sicilian Vespers against the Angevins of Naples – the Aragonese of Spain strongly repressed Sicilian aspirations to autonomy. Andrea Chiaramonte, the only one of the four Vicars who resisted the troops of Martin of Aragon, was captured and beheaded in Piano della Marina, the square below his sumptuous Palermitan palace, the *Steri*, which can still be admired today. In 1415 the Crown of Sicily was joined to the Spanish Crown of Aragon; the island was thus ruled by viceroys and enjoyed a period of relative peace. The viceroys resided first in the Chiaramonte fam-

"Madonna della Scala" by Antonello Gagini (16C), in the Sacristy of Palermo Cathedral.

ily's *Steri*, later in the Castellammare fortress and finally in the ancient Royal Palace.

In the 14C, due to the Vespers War and to baronial anarchy, Sicily withdrew into itself, and the art it produced was a mere continuation of the expressive forms which had characterized the previous age. Palermo's 14C architecture has been called "chiaramontana" due to the strong influence which this aristocratic family had on the city's artistic life. This was also the century of the great feudal castles, which took on their final architectural forms. The Chiaramonte family owned the castles of Caccamo and Carini, both in the vicinity of Palermo, as well as the massive Palermitan palace known as *Steri* (from *Hosterium* = Hostel). These fortified buildings similar to royal palaces – the most representative examples being the *Steri* and Palazzo Sclafani, though many others exist – have inlaid decorative motifs and original intertwined arches which bear witness to a reinterpretation of the previous tradition by 14C craftsmen.

15C art was characterized by the so-called "Sicilian Gothic" style, bearing Catalan influences. The most outstanding architect of the time was Matteo Carnalivari of Noto, to whom the elegant Church of Santa Maria della Catena, in the Cala quarter, has been attributed. Carnalivari also designed Palazzo Abatellis

Castellammare Fortress. In the foreground, the remains of the San Giorgio Bastion (16C). In the background, the San Pietro Bastion (15C).

(which now houses the Sicilian Regional Gallery) and Palazzo Aiutamicristo (1490), two of the most magnificent examples of 15C urban aristocratic residences in Italy. In 1468, Piazza Ballarò was laid out – this was a wide road (a *Platea*) designed to create a more spacious area for a large market – as well as the elegant Via Porta di Termini (the present-day Via Garibaldi), overlooked by Palazzo Aiutamicristo. In the following century, this palace was the residence of Charles V and Don Juan of Austria. Between the 15C and 16C, new impulse was given to the neglected Palermitan sculpture by the workshops of the Gaginis, a family of skilful sculptors and stucco decorators (including Domenico, Antonello and a host of relatives). The Gaginis did not confine their work to sculpturing single statues of Madonnas and Saints, but inserted them into magnificent architectural ensembles, enriched with frames, panels, balustrades depicting stories of the Saints and delicate decorative motifs, which embellished church apses and chapels, thus introducing Tuscan Renaissance taste into Palermo.

Between the 15C and 16C, Greek and Albanian refugees arrived in Sicily, fleeing from their countries after the Ottoman invasion. Most of them settled in the mountains overlooking Palermo. At Piana degli Albanesi, Mezzojuso, Palazzo Adriano, Santa Cristina Gela and Contessa Entellina there are still numerous Albanian-speaking groups, and Byzantine religious rites are celebrated. Under Charles V and later under Don Juan of Austria, Sicily became the naval base from which the Italo-Spanish imperial recovery against Muslim expansionism started. Palermo added new bastions and strongholds to its walls, and strengthened both the Cala, with the construction of the South Dock (1545), and the Castellammare (the ancient *Castrum Inferius*), according to plans by the royal architect Antonio Ferramolino. In 1567, the New Dock (or North Dock) was begun, a construction which was admired by all European navies.

In the 16C, the first town-planning reforms were implemented, with the creation of a number of squares and streets designed to make life more comfortable for the citizens, and the running of the city's various activities easier. In 1510, Piazza della Foglia or Bocceria Grande (*Vucciria*) was completed to facilitate the organization of both the street market and the trading activities of the "nations", i.e. the settlements of Amalfitans, Catalans, Genoese, etc. Piazza del Garraffello was laid out for the same purpose between 1545 and 1549. New town-planning reforms, launched by the viceroyal administration, changed Palermo's aspect: in 1581 the city's main artery, the *Cassaro* (the present-day Corso V. Emanuele), was straightened and extended as far as the seafront by Viceroy Marco Antonio Colonna. Previously, in 1577, the "piano a mare" (i.e. promenade, the present-day Foro Italico) had been completed, with the creation of a street named after the viceroy of the time: Strada Colonna. Private town-planning initiatives were first taken by the powerful Bologna family, who created a large square along the Cassaro, called Piano dei Bologna (now Piazza Bologni).

Church of San Francesco D'Assisi

The church stands in Piazza San Francesco and can be reached from the Cassaro (Corso V. Emanuele) through Via Alessandro Paternostro. It was built between 1266 and 1277, after the return to

Church of San Francesco d'Assisi. Façade and detail of the entrance portal.

Church of San Francesco d'Assisi. Nave.

Palermo of the Franciscans, who had on several occasions been sent away by the royal and ecclesiastical authorities. The building proportionally reproduces the "mixed" plan inaugurated by Palermo and Monreale Cathedrals, the Palatine Chapel and especially the Church of Santo Spirito, thus reflecting the attachment of the city's craftsmen to the architectural tradition of the Hauteville age. The church has undergone numerous alterations, as shown by some of the existing elements. The 13C construction, in fact, was first altered in the 15C, when Renaissance features were added by Domenico Gagini and Francesco Laurana. Further alterations were carried out in the 17C, when the old wooden ceiling was replaced by cross vaulting. Between the 17C and 18C, the interior was decorated with Novelli's

frescoes and numerous stuccoes, including those executed by Serpotta. Restoration work, begun in 1824 after a devastating earthquake, introduced the forms of the new neoclassical taste. The church was restored after being damaged by bombing during the last World War and eventually regained its austere 14C aspect. The façade is the feature which, more than the rest, has maintained its original aspect in spite of all the alterations made over the centuries. Together with the exquisite Gothic portal (built later than 1302), it was restored to its organic unity by the architect Patricolo in the 19C. The architect also reconstructed the central rose window, in keeping with the design of its counterpart in the Church of Sant'Agostino. The marble columns flanking the portal bear the coats of arms of the Chiaramonte and Abatellis families, who financed the construction. The small columns support elegant archivolts with the characteristic zigzag motif introduced throughout 14C Sicily by the "chiaramontano" style. Between the rose window and the portal is a small and elegant three-niche pediment, with frescoes dating from later ages. The two minor portals are in Renaissance style. The most significant works in the interior include the portal of the chapel dedicated to the Madonna della Neve, which also houses a Madonna and Child and the Madonna della Grazia by Domenico Gagini; the Mastrantonio Chapel by Francesco Laurana; and the Vision of St Francis, a fresco by Pietro Novelli transferred onto canvas. In the sober Renaissance presbytery are the famous stuccoed female figures depicting Humility, Faith, Meekness, Modesty, Theology, Charity, Truth and Fortitude by Serpotta, who also executed those in the nave.

Church of San Francesco d'Assisi. Statue of Modesty (by Giacomo Serpotta, 17C-18C).

Church of Sant'Agostino

The south flank of the church looks onto via Sant'Agostino, while the façade overlooks via Maestri d'Acqua. The present-day building was erected in the second half of the 13C, probably in 1295, on the site of a pre-existing church. The façade dates from the early 14C and was financed by the Sclafani and Chiaramonte families. The central portal is decorated with arabesques and abstract or floral stylized motifs in lava pumice. Above the apex of the pediment is a circular rose window, with 12 white marble mullions and the central roundel depicting the *Agnus Dei*. The façade also bears the coats of arms of the Chiaramonte and Sclafani families. The lateral portal is probably a Gaginesque work by Giuliano Mancino and Bartolomeo Berrettaro. The single-nave interior is the result of alterations carried out in the 17C-18C. It houses stuccoes by Serpotta and other remarkable works including the bust of Francesco Medici, by Ignazio Marabitti (18C), and a painting by Giuseppe Salerno, known as "lo Zoppo di Gangi" (17C), depicting stories of St Tommaso Villanova. The 16C cloister was also rebuilt on the site of a pre-existing cloister. On the internal walls are frescoes depicting the life of St Augustine.

The Chiaramonte family's Steri *palace, now housing the Rectorate of the University of Palermo.*

Palazzo Chiaramonte (the "Steri")

The building, popularly known as the Steri, from the Latin *Hosterium* (Hostel), stands at the east corner of Piazza Marina. The Chiaramonte family's palace was designed as a typical medieval aristocratic residence, its severe and massive structure reflecting the power of the original owners. The palace, with an internal courtyard featuring a lower portico and upper loggia, is also one of the first, prestigious examples of aristocratic residences in Italy. Between the 13C and 14C, the Chiaramonte family attained considerable power, thanks to their vast estates scattered throughout the island. Here they built a large number of castles, palaces and churches, all conceived and carried out in a uniform architectural style. Work on the *Steri* was begun in 1306 by Manfredi I and was completed around 1380 by Manfredi III, Count of Modica. Following the political decline of the family, the building was confiscated by Martin I of Aragon and became the residence of the kings of the Aragonese dynasty of Sicily, and later of the viceroys. At the beginning of the 17C, it became the seat of the Court of the Holy Office (the Inquisition), and its interior underwent a number of alterations. The first *autos-da-*

fé (the burning of the heretics condemned by the Inquisition) took place in front of the *Steri*, in Piano della Marina. Drawings, graffiti, rough paintings and writings by unknown prisoners of the Court of the Inquisition have been found in the prison cells. The palace finally became the seat of the Courts and of the Customs' Office. After recent restoration work, it now houses the Rectorate of the University of Palermo. The front overlooking the square has large two- and three-light windows, elegantly decorated with the characteristic inlaid work, which reflect the Sicilian architectural tradition of the Middle Ages. From the courtyard, a staircase leads up to the Sala Magna, whose wooden ceiling with coffers is the largest painted ceiling still bearing witness to the sumptuousness of these structural and decorative elements. The ceiling, with its geometric decorations and skilfully executed pictorial cycles, is the work of different artists: Cecco di Naro, Simone da Corleone and Dareno da Palermo, who painted stories from the Old Testament, legends of chivalry, popular episodes, scenes of everyday life and themes extolling the Chiaramonte family. Adjoining the palace is the Chiaramonte Chapel, or Chapel of Sant'Antonio Abate, characterized by a simple façade and a relief-decorated portal.

The Chiaramonte family's Steri *palace. Two-light window in the façade, lavishly decorated with lava stone inlays typical of Sicilian 14C architecture.*

Palazzo Sclafani

The palace stands in Piazzetta San Giovanni Decollato, which can be entered from the east corner of Piazza Vittoria. It was built by Matteo Sclafani, Count of Adernò, to compete with his brother-in-law Chiaramonte, who had previously built the *Steri*. It is unlikely that the building was erected in less than a year (in 1330), as was indicated in a memorial tablet formerly embedded in the east front of the palace and no longer extant. Of the ancient building – used as a hospital in the 15C and transformed into a barracks in 1852 – only the south front has retained its original aspect, while the north and west fronts have undergone substantial renovation. With its regular prismatic structure and spacious courtyard featuring a lower portico and upper loggia, the palace further testifies to the refinement of 14C Palermitan civil architecture, which clearly heralded the later architectural models of central Italy. In the internal quadrangular courtyard, which has undergone substantial alterations, was the fresco depicting "The Triumph of Death", now on exhibition at the Regional Gallery in Palazzo Abatellis. The south front has a splendid portal topped by an elegantly decorated niche with the coats of arms of the Sclafani family, the city, Sicily and Aragon. The upper floor is characterized by large intertwined arches decorated with lava stone inlays, typical of 14C architecture.

Archbishop's Palace and Seminary

Between Via Matteo Bonello and Corso Vittorio Emanuele stands the Archbishop's Palace and the old Seminary. The two buildings, erected in different periods, were joined into a single structure in the mid-18C. In the Middle Ages, the Archbishop's Palace was situated next to the three apses of the Cathedral, in accordance with a hierarchical principle based on the predominance of the apsidal area vis-à-vis the over-

Archbishop's Palace. East front looking onto the square.

all architectural aspect of a church. As Via del Cassaro became increasingly more important in the urban layout of 15C Palermo, Archbishop Simone Bologna decided to build the new Archbishop's Palace between this street and the Cathedral, in a privileged position. The new archiepiscopal residence was erected in the 15C. The only remaining elements of the main front dating from that age, however, are an elegant three-light window and the main portal, with a segmental arch bearing the coat of arms of the Bologna family. The Palace houses the Diocesan Museum, founded in 1927. The Seminary Palace, overlooking Piazza Vittoria, is a late-16C work by the architect Giorgio Di Faccio, but it underwent several alterations in the 17C and 18C. One of the balconies looking onto the square was carved by Vincenzo Gagini.

Church of Santa Maria degli Angeli, known as the "Gancia"

The church is in Via Alloro, next to Palazzo Abatellis. Both the monastery and the church were built at the beginning of the 16C by the Franciscans of Santa Maria di Gesù, a village near Palermo, as a "Gancia" (lodging, hospice) for travelling friars. The church has a 15C simple and essential architecture, as is evident in the façade and in the side front, which is surrounded by a railing. On the portal arch is a delicate bas-relief of the Madonna. The interior has a single nave, with a series of side chapels and round (originally ogival) arches. Stuccoes by Serpotta embellish some of the chapels; over the high altar is the Holy Family and, in the third chapel to the left, San Pietro d'Alcantara, both ascribed to Pietro Novelli. In the Presbytery and in the sixth chapel to the left are some relief works by Gagini. At the entrance is a great 16C organ ascribable to Raffaele La Valle. The adjoining monastery, which can be entered from Piazzetta della Gancia, features a loggia in late-15C style which was part of the original construction. In the courtyard is a graceful baroque well. Next to the church, in Via Alloro, is the so-called "safety hole", through which some patriots, who had taken refuge in the monastery after the failure of the revolt of April 1860, managed to escape.

Church of Santa Maria degli Angeli. Nave.

Church of Santa Maria degli Angeli. Covering of the central apse.

Church of Santa Maria dei Miracoli

On the south corner of Piazza Marina is the church of Santa Maria dei Miracoli, the work of Fazio Gagini, built on the site where a wall painting of the Virgin Mary was believed to have miraculous powers. The rectangular façade is decorated with pilaster strips and a Renaissance pediment. The interior, of great formal and spatial elegance, is quadrangular in plan, with a nave and two aisles, modelled on the original plan of the Church of Santa Maria dell'Ammiraglio (Martorana). The cornices, capitals and holy water stoup are works of the Gaginesque school.

Church of San Giorgio dei Genovesi

The church, built to a design by the architect Giorgio Di Faccio, stands in the square of the same name, which can be entered from Via Squarcialupo. It was erected for the confraternity of San Giorgio dei Genovesi, i.e. on the orders of the members of the Genoese "nation" (settlement). Completed in the 16C – at least the main structures – it is one of the rare examples of Renaissance architecture in Palermo to have maintained its original forms. The 18C gilded stuccoes which decorated the presbytery were removed during restoration work carried out at the end of the 19C. The interior has 16C and 17C paintings from different schools.

Church of San Giorgio dei Genovesi, façade. The external round window framed by a cartouche.

Palazzo Abatellis

Palazzo Abatellis, now housing the Sicilian Regional Gallery. The internal courtyard with the elegant portico and upper loggia.

The palace, situated in Via Alloro, has been the seat of the Sicilian Regional Gallery since 1954, after adequate restoration work. It was built in 1495 for the Palermitan

aristocrat Francesco Patella, who held the office of "Maestro Portolano del Regno" (i.e. he was in charge of the commercial port) during the reign of King Ferdinand "the Catholic". The building was designed by Matteo Carnalivari in the elegant architectural forms of the Sicilian 15C style. Both the spatial arrangement, planned around a vast inner atrium embellished by an elegant portico with an upper loggia, and the refined decoration of the portal and external windows are worthy of note. The three-light panelled windows are ornamented with slender mullions and intertwined decorative patterns.

Palazzo Aiutamicristo

The palace, situated in Via Garibaldi, was erected between 1490 and 1495 to a design by Carnalivari. It has been extensively altered and is now in disrepair, but its imposing 15C façade overlooking Via Garibaldi and the courtyard has been preserved fairly intact. The courtyard reflects the layout typical of Carnalivari's palaces. The ground-floor portico features segmental arches, while the upper loggia consists of a series of pointed arches. In addition to the monumental and elegant entrance portal, there are several pointed or round-arched minor portals.

Church of Santa Maria della Catena

The church stands between Corso V. Emanuele and the Cala, on the north-eastern corner of Piazza Marina. It was built on the site of an older chapel which had existed as early as the time of Frederick (I of Sicily; II of the Empire) and was also called "della Catena" (of the Chain). In fact, the ancient port in front of the church lay between two rocky spurs, so close to each other that the narrow entrance to the port could be blocked by a heavy chain, as was customary in ancient times to prevent night naval attacks. In the 16C, the old church was demolished and the new one was built, financed by the believers, King Martin and Queen Mary of Aragon.

Church of Santa Maria della Catena. Façade and (bottom) nave.

It is still controversial whether the design can be entirely attributed to Matteo Carnalivari. This is the last church built in accordance with the Palermitan "mixed" plan of medieval origin (Monreale and Palermo Cathedrals, Santa Maria Maddalena, Santo Spirito, San Francesco), in which a basilican body consisting of a nave and two aisles is inserted into a portion of a centrally planned body corresponding to the three-apsidal Sanctuary. This original layout has been altered by the presence of two rows of chapels which were later added to the sides of the aisles. The design of the individual architectural elements is extremely elegant and gives the interior a unique atmosphere of serenity and formal purity. Several additions have been made to the church, including the front portico, the side chapels and numerous baroque features which were removed during restoration work carried out in the post-war period. In the entrance portico, three portals with bas-reliefs attributed to Vincenzo Gagini lead into the church. The only remaining baroque elements – dating from the time of the Theatine Fathers' administration – are the decorations of the right-side chapels, a number of sarcophagi and a painting in the right apse, attributed to Novelli. The church houses 16C works, including four Gaginesque statues of saints and a bas-relief of the Coronation of the Virgin in the third chapel on the right.

Church of the Spasimo. Nave and apse.

Church of the "Spasimo"

This is a rather unusual but fascinating monument, situated in the *Kalsa* quarter. Although essentially hybrid in style, it is the only example of "Gothic-like" architecture in Palermo (see the Sanctuary area). Both the church and monastery were built in 1509 for the Olivetan Fathers who, however, were forced to leave it in 1573 due to the construction of a "cavalier" tower in the adjacent Spasimo Bastion, which was part of the city walls. The church housed a famous painting by Raphael – the Madonna dello Spasimo – which was given to King Philip IV in 1661 and is now displayed at the Prado Museum in Madrid. The city's Senate used the complex as a poorhouse and, after 1858, as a hospital, while the large church served as a warehouse. The building is now roofless, as the original wooden covering of the nave and of part of the central Sanctuary is missing. The far end of the Sanctuary – of impressive height – is covered with ribbed vaults. The former church, recently restored, is now used for artistic and musical performances and conferences.

Church of the Spasimo. The massive but ruined covering structures.

Ancient street markets

Palermo's origin as a commercial emporium has influenced the economic and social life of the city for centuries, and street markets have always been the living (and lively) proof of this ancient commercial tradition. For this reason, they are an interesting "mirror of life" for the tourist who wants to discover all the different aspects of this multifaceted city. The earliest records on Palermitan street markets date from the beginning of the 14C, although they were probably created earlier. The seaport markets were closely connected to the arrival of goods by sea, mainly spices, textiles and raw materials. They were partly controlled by the fiduciaries of the Maritime Republics (Amalfitans, Genoese, Pisans), who administered the "fondaci" (warehouses where goods were both stored and sold). Later, these markets passed under the control of the great seafaring nations: the Catalans in the 16C and the English in the early 19C, albeit in a different way. The warehouses were thus situated around the Cala, particularly in the Loggia quarter. This was also the residential area of the so-called "Nations", i.e. the communities of merchants from outside Sicily who had set up their commercial bases in Palermo.

The name *Bocceria* (or *Vucciria*) derives from the French word *Boucherie*, i.e. place for the sale of meat. We do not know whether the area took this name in the 12C or during the Angevin rule in the 13C, when French was spoken at Court and in the military and commercial milieux of the island. The urban layout of the *Vucciria* as we know it today is the result of one of the first town-planning reforms in Palermo. The present-day Piazza del Garraffello, which is still the heart of the *Vucciria*, was formerly called Piano della Loggia. In fact, from the 15C onwards, the square was the seat of the Loggias, i.e. the places equipped with a "tavola" (bank) where the "foreign nations" carried out their business transactions. The square was also important because it was the seat of the "Tavola e Banco Pubblico", the public bank of the city, which was moved to the Town Hall (or Senatorial Palace) in 1617. Between 1545 and 1549 the square was systematically renovated by the Palermitan Senate, on account of its commercial importance. The Garraffello Fountain was placed here in 1591, giving its name to the square. Between 1454 and 1510, the

Fishmonger's stall in the Capo market. The food markets in the old city centre are always abounding with fish.

square of the *Bocceria Grande* was laid out with a view to enhancing the "*decorazione et bellezza*" (decoration and beauty) of the area. Following the decline of the Cala and the building of the new naval port in the northern part of the city, near the Acquasanta quarter, the *Bocceria* lost its "seaport" element. However, it maintained its "internal" or local function, and its vitality. The market was later named *Bocceria della Foglia* to indicate that fruit and vegetables (formerly called *foglia*, i.e. leaf) were sold. In 1783, the main square was systematically renovated by Viceroy Caracciolo, and surrounded by porticoes. With the creation of Via Roma at the end of the 19C, Piazza Caracciolo, named after the viceroy, became narrower and the porticoes were demolished. The square is now at the edge of a larger market which has extended to the surrounding streets.

The "internal" markets mostly served the purpose of gathering together the foodstuffs from the rich and fertile countryside around Palermo for daily sale. The most lively among these have always been the *Ballarò* and *Capo* markets. The name *Ballarò* seems to have derived from the fact that fruit and vegetables from an area near Monreale, called Balara, were sold in this part of the city. *Ballarò* was also the first quarter of the city that one crossed when entering through the Sant'Agata Gate. In more recent times, the original fruit and vegetable market has opened out to other products, including meat, textiles, shoes and clothing, and even coffins. As in the case of the *Bocceria*, the present layout of the centre of the *Ballarò* market is the result of a town-planning regulation issued by the Palermitan Senate. The systematic arrangement of the square was begun in 1468 and continued in successive stages. This strange square – in fact, it is a wide and short street – was originally a *platea* (from the Greek *plateia* = wide street) of the *Deinsin* quarter, where retailers and buyers crowded together within a very small area. Later architectural works, such as the 17C Church of the Carmine by Mariano Smiriglio, have created a suggestive urban scene, but they will not be discussed in detail here.

The large *Capo* market consists of an intricate network of minor streets leading out into the main roads and crowded with people doing their shopping. Today it is mainly a food market (fruit and vegetables, meat, fish). The area occupied by the market cor-

Gorgeous fruit and vegetable stall in the Vucciria market. The liveliness of this market combines with the colourfulness of the exhibited goods.

responds to the upper part of the ancient *Seracaldio* quarter, which extended from *Dainisinni* to the sea along the Sant'Agostino-Via Bandiera road axis. The name *Capo* probably derives from the ancient name of the area, *Caput Seracaldii.*

On 3 November 1508, Viceroy Raimondo de Cordova issued two town-planning regulations concerning the street known as Discesa dei Giudici, as far as the Church of Sant'Anna, and Via Lattarini, which was the site of another lively market. The *Lattarini* market (which is thought to have originally dealt in spices) is now situated between Via Roma and Via Alessandro Paternostro. The original quarter of the market consisted of the area bounded by the Church of San Nicolò da Tolentino, in Via Maqueda, and the squares of Sant'Anna and Cassa di Risparmio, to the seaward side of Via Roma, a few yards before the crossroads with Corso V. Emanuele. The creation of the second section of Via Roma, at the beginning of the 20C, altered the ancient road layout of the quarter. Today, in the main road – Via Lattarini, which takes its name from the original quarter – as well as in the surrounding streets, you can still find shops and stalls selling clothes, arms, ironware, cloth and cordage.

There was also another type of market, which still flourishes today: the art- and craftwork market. Traces of this are still evident in the names of many streets: Via dei

Cintorinai (belt-makers), Calderai (copperpot-makers), Argentieri (silversmiths), Biscottari (biscuit-makers), Bottai (coopers), Candelai (candle-makers), Cappellieri (hatters), and many others (Chiavettieri, Lettighieri, Pannieri...). The workshops along these streets often manufactured the same kind of articles: this contributed to the liveliness of the market and made shopping easier and more convenient for the population. Some streets and alleys still retain the name of the craftsmen who used to work there: hence Via Argenteria Nuova and Via Argenteria Vecchia were named after the goldsmiths and silversmiths who had their workshops there, especially in the 17C-18C, and today both Via Argenteria Vecchia and the surrounding streets have a large number of jeweller's shops. Via dei Cassari owes its name to the makers of crates ("casse"), oars and ladders; Via dei Maccheronai, to the shops where women made various kinds of pasta. Via dei Formai was named after the makers of lasts ("forme") who had their shops there. Today, this market is in the heart of the old city centre, in a quadrilateral bounded by Via Roma, Piazza San Domenico, the Cala and Corso Vittorio Emanuele.

In the great market quarters, the gradual occupation of the roads and of the surrounding buildings by the vendors was due to the fact that their activity was not confined to the sale of products, but also included manufacture, and repair of used or damaged articles, so that the markets were at the same time an enormous workshop. The buildings in the area were all involved in the various stages of production, in addition to being used as warehouses. This invasion of public areas must have given rise to frequent conflicts with the local authorities. In 1544, the Marquis of Terranova, who presided over the Kingdom, issued a decree in favour of the "decorum and ornamentation" of the city, in which he denounced the fact that the roadways in the market quarters were considerably narrowed by the presence of stalls, ordering the demolition of those designed as permanent structures. He also decreed that goods should be kept in the shops and not outside. But the fate of the decree is not difficult to imagine. Palermo's ancient street markets have retained all their liveliness up to the present day, as a walk around them will clearly show.

THE AGE OF THE VICEROYS AND OF THE RELIGIOUS ORDERS (16th-18th centuries)

In the 17C, the city's defensive system was finally completed. The Castellammare was equipped with massive bulwarks and the city walls were strengthened by thirteen bastions, of which only those of the Spasimo (between Piazza Magione and Via Lincoln), Royal Palace (overlooking Piazza Indipendenza) and Papireto (in Corso Alberto Amedeo) remain today. The coastal blockhouses, built in the 17C, have also been demolished. Only a few watchtowers – once used for signalling the arrival of the enemy by sea – are still scattered along the coast (Arenella, Acquasanta, Rotoli, Acqua dei Corsari, etc.).

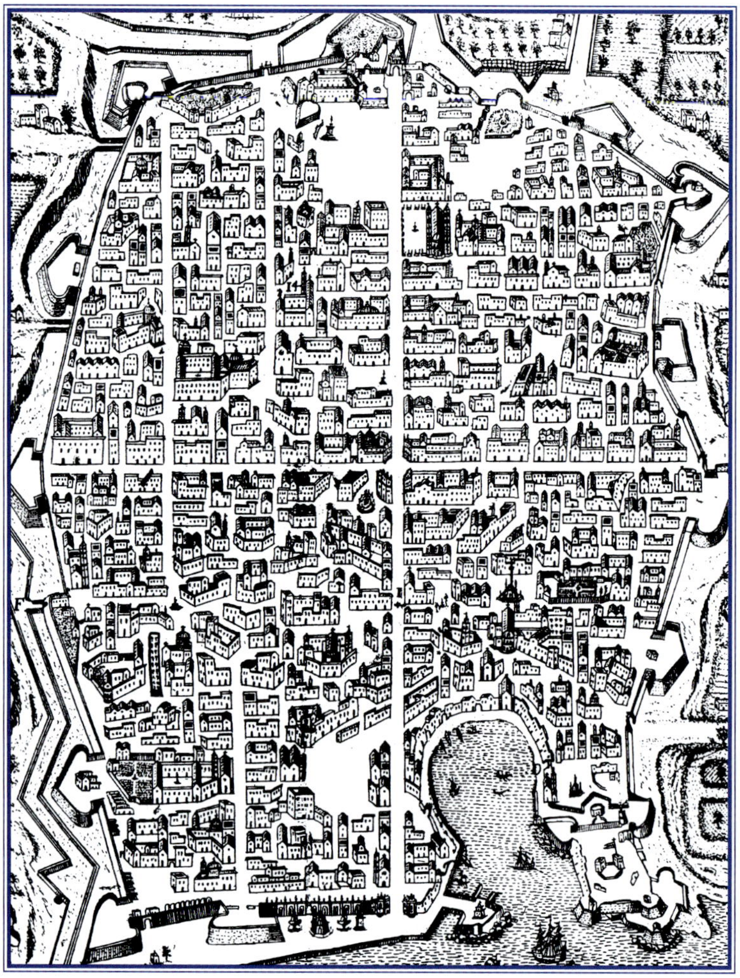

Palermo, detail of the city plan, from an engraving by Antonino Bova (1732).

In this period (17C and 18C), Palermo's architectural activity was promoted not only by the Crown and the Senate, but also by two important groups of clients: the Aristocracy and the great religious Orders. These Orders entrusted their architects (who had been the disciples of the masters of Mannerism and Baroque in Rome) with the design of religious houses, churches, convents and monasteries. All these buildings contributed to Palermo's architectural grandeur: Casa Professa dei Gesuiti, San Giuseppe dei Teatini, Santa Teresa alla Kalsa, San Domenico, San Francesco Saverio, Sant'Anna. The architects Angelo Italia, Lorenzo Ciprì and Andrea Giganti were Jesuits; Tommaso Napoli, Andrea Cirrincione and Benedetto del Castrone were Dominicans; Giacomo Amato was a Crutched friar; Giacomo Besio, a Theatine; Paolo Amato, the designer of some of the most beautiful Triumphal Chariots of St Rosalia, belonged to the Congregation of the "Padri Ministri degli Infermi"; Giovan Biagio Amico was a priest. At this time, the prevailing style in the architecture of churches, religious houses and palaces was not – as many believe – Baroque, but Mannerism. The priest-architects, in fact, imported from Rome this aesthetic current which appealed to the great clients and reflected the taste of Palermo's elite. The city thus became the second capital of Roman Mannerism. Baroque taste was limited only to the internal decoration of most of the churches and of some of the palaces. Church interiors, in particular, were sumptuously decorated with polychrome marble inlays, stuccoed human figures and ornamental motifs, skilfully executed ironwork, polychrome floors, not to mention paintings and furnishings. In sculpture, Palermo outclassed the rest of Italy with the greatest stucco decorator of all time: Giacomo Serpotta (1656-1732), the author of the magnificent stuccoes in the Oratories of Santa Cita, the Rosario and San Lorenzo. His work was continued by his son Procopio and by numerous disciples. Great names in painting were those of Pietro Novelli (1603-1647), Filippo Paladini, Vito d'Anna, Antonino Grano.

In the 17C-18C, the aristocratic families – thanks to the large profits obtained from their farm estates in the hinterland – moved to the capital, building sumptuous palaces

which were unrivalled in Europe. The Villafranca, Ugo, Belmonte and Riso palaces were erected in Piazza Bologni, Palermo's aristocratic showcase. The majestic Palazzo Trabia rose along the Marina promenade. An entire new street, the *Strada Nova* (the present-day Via Maqueda) was started in 1600 to allow the building of new aristocratic palaces (the most important being Palazzo Comitini) along the road axis which runs perpendicular to the former Via del *Cassaro* (now Via Vittorio Emanuele). At the crossroads of the *Strada Nova* and the *Cassaro*, Piazza Vigliena was laid out (also known

Cathedral interior. Engraving by Antonino Bova, from D. Schiavo "Descrizione della solenne acclamazione e del giuramento di fedeltà al Re di Sicilia Ferdinando Borbone", Palermo 1760.

as the Octagon, the Theatre of the Sun, or the Four Corners of the City), the heart of 17C-18C Palermo. The city was divided into four large districts or "Mandamenti": Albergheria (patron saint St Christine); Capo (patron saint St Ninfa); Kalsa (patron saint St Agatha) and Loggia (patron saint St Oliva).

At either end of the Cassaro, two gates – Porta Nuova and Porta Felice – were the finishing touches to this urban layout. Meanwhile, particularly in the 18C, great villas were built in the countryside around Palermo. The most important group of these residences is in Bagheria: Villa Palagonia, Villa Butera, Villa Cattolica, Villa Trabia, Villa Inguaggiato. Other villas were built in the plain below Monreale and in Piana dei Colli, where a large number of country houses (*bagli* and *casene*) sprang up: the Airoldi, Amari, Bordonaro, Boscogrande, Castelnuovo, De Cordova, Lampedusa, Maniscalco, Pantelleria, Ranchibile, Scalea, Spina and Trabia villas. Some of the ancient feudal castles surrounding the capital of the viceroyalty were transformed into aristocratic palaces, a symbol of the changed social and political conditions.

At this time, public festivals – both lay and religious – were at the height of their splendour in Palermo, also thanks to the rich scenographic ensembles, to the external decorations of churches and palaces, to the magnificent Triumphal Chariots of St Rosalia and to the "firework display machines". Among the best-known designers of

these scenographic apparatuses were the architects of the Palermitan Senate, Paolo Amato and Andrea Palma. Great Italian and foreign travellers and men of culture (Goethe, Brydone, Houel and others) described the splendour of these festivals in tones of wonder and astonishment.

At the beginning of the 18C, Palermo had a population of 100,000, the same as Rome, Lisbon and Amsterdam. In the same period, Naples had 250,000 inhabitants. In 1723, Palermo had 107 princes, 76 dukes, 104 marquises, 39 counts, 1 viscount, and 484 barons. Following the Peace of Vienna (1738), Charles of Bourbon, the son of Emperor Philip V, became king of Sicily, Naples and the Spanish duchies in Tuscany. The reign of the Bourbons of Naples thus began, and Sicily was ruled first by their viceroys, and then by lieutenants. The seat of the viceroys was always Palermo. King Charles of Bourbon built the great architectural complex of the Albergo delle Povere (a poorhouse) and other public works. At the end of the 18C, following the invasion of the Kingdom by French troops, King Ferdinand of Bourbon (III of Sicily and IV of Naples) was twice forced to leave Naples for Palermo, where he stayed for a few years. Here he promoted the architectural renovation of the Cathedral, the restoration of the Royal Palace and other works. He also created the famous Favorita Park, where the "Palazzina Cinese" (Chinese Palace) stands, and the Ficuzza royal wood near Corleone. In 1812, King Ferdinand sanctioned the Sicilian Constitution which (on paper) abolished the feudal system; in 1816, he restored the Kingdom of the Two Sicilies, with Naples as capital, changing his name to Ferdinand I of the Two Sicilies. The most distinguished architect between the 18C and 19C was Venanzio Marvuglia, who designed the Riso, Geraci, Costantino and Coglitore palaces, the Oratory of San Filippo Neri, Villa Belmonte and the Palazzina Cinese.

Fontana delle Vergogne in Piazza Pretoria. The sumptuously scenographic design of the fountain is enhanced by the buildings in the background.

The Fountain of Piazza Pretoria

The square, an irregular quadrangle in shape, was named after the Town Hall ("Pretorio"), also called Palazzo delle Aquile (i.e. the Palace of Eagles) because of the eagles sculptured in its cornice. It lies in the heart of the old city centre, between the Quattro Canti di Città and Piazza Bellini. The monumental fountain in the centre of the square has had a rather complicated history. Designed and built to embellish a sumptuous Florentine villa, following the death of the original client it remained incomplete and disassembled for years, until the Palermitan Senate bought it for 20,000 scudi, stirring up a scandal. The fountain was built in the 16C to a design by the

Fontana delle Vergogne.
A picturesque view by night.

Tuscan architects Camilliani and Naccherini. It has a circular layout with concentric basins arranged on three levels, culminating in the central fountain. The basins are surrounded by statues, mostly representing pagan deities and animal figures. Since most of the statues depict naked male and female bodies, the Palermitans began to call it "Fontana delle Vergogne" (Fountain of Shame), a name which was eventually extended to the square. The fountain, one of the finest 16C monuments adorning the city, is further embellished by the play of light and water set up in the evening and night hours.

Quattro Canti
(the Octagon, the Theatre of the Sun, or Piazza Vigliena)

This was the most sumptuous monumental crossroads to be created in Europe in the early 17C. From that period through the 19C, it was the geometric centre of the city. The four architectural façades are a clear expression of the idea of imperial power they were designed to convey. The architectural complex was also called "Teatro del Sole" (Theatre of the Sun) because at any time during the day at least one of the four corners will be lit up by sunshine. It was built to a design by the royal architect Giulio Lasso, while the plastic decoration is the work of Mariano Smiriglio, an architect of the Senate. Construction began in 1608 and was completed in 1620. The sculptures adorning each façade are arranged as follows: on the lower level, above the basins, is the personification of one of the four Seasons; in the middle is the statue of a sovereign; on the upper level is the patron saint of the Mandamento (district) associated with that corner; at the top is an imperial eagle with the coats of arms of the Spanish kingdom, the city and the viceroys. Starting from the north-east in a clockwise direction, the statues represent, from bottom to top: Autumn, Philip IV, St Oliva (north corner); Winter, Philip III, St Agatha (east corner); Spring, Charles V, St Christine (south corner); Summer, Philip II, St Ninfa (west corner). St Rosalia is not depicted as she was proclaimed patron saint of the city only in 1624.

Top: Piazza Vigliena. East Corner of the Quattro Canti.

Bottom: Piazza Vigliena. Allegorical statue of Summer above the fountain of the west Corner.

Oratory of the Rosario near the Church of Santa Cita. The Battle of Lepanto.

Church of Santa Cita and Oratory of the Rosario

The church, which stands between Via Valverde and Via Squarcialupo, was built between 1586 and 1603 on the site of a 15C church also dedicated to St Cita. The late-Renaissance façade was completed in 1781. The interior contains notable sculptures by Antonello Gagini, which formerly adorned the 15C church. At the end of the presbytery is the marble arch of St Cita, depicting episodes from the life of the Saint, the Nativity and, on the pilaster strips, Dominican saints in meditation. In the second chapel to the left of the presbytery is the sarcophagus of Antonio Scirotta, also the work of Antonello Gagini. To the right of the presbytery is the Rosario Chapel, purely baroque in style, with variegated marble ornamentation and sculptures by Gioacchino Vitaliano, depicting the ten Mysteries of the Rosary. The Oratory is to the left of the church, in Via Valverde. The building, architecturally very simple, was erected in the 17C and entirely decorated by Serpotta between 1685 and 1718, the main theme of the ornamentation being the ten Mysteries of the Rosary. On the back wall are panels framing groups of small statues, similar to wax models, which depict the Resurrection and the Ascension on one side, the Pentecost and the Assumption on the other. In the middle is the Coronation of the Virgin and, above, a relief celebrating the battle of Lepanto, which was won thanks to the intercession of the Madonna of the Rosary. Above the high altar is a painting of the Madonna of the Rosary by Carlo Marotta; along the walls are splendid choir-stalls decorated with mother-of-pearl inlays.

Oratory of the Rosario near the Church of Santa Cita. A picturesque view of the whole.

Church of Sant'Ignazio all'Olivella

The church, which stands in the square of the same name, was built for the Congregation of St Filippo Neri. It was begun in 1598 and completed in 1622. The 18C dome, internally decorated with geometric patterns, was designed by Venanzio Marvuglia. The interior features the sumptuous Chapel of the Crucifix, with a rich ornamentation of jasper columns (in the altar), agate, amethyst, lapis lazuli, topaz and oriental garnet. In the chapel vault is a small fresco by Pietro Novelli; above the altar is the Archangel Gabriel, also by Novelli. Behind the high altar are two statues depicting St Peter and St Paul, by Marabitti. To the right of the church is the Oratory of Sant'Ignazio all'Olivella, built in 1769 to a design by the architect Venanzio Marvuglia. The Angel in the presbytery is the work of Ignazio Marabitti.

Top: Church of Sant'Ignazio all'Olivella. Façade.

Casa Professa

The building can be reached from Via Maqueda by way of Via Casa Professa, which leads to the square of the same name. Its name derives from the Jesuit Fathers, also called "Padri Professi" (Professed Fathers) because they had taken the four religious vows. Construction began in 1564, when the Abbey of Santa Maria della Cerotta and the surrounding buildings were massively restored to provide an adequate seat for the religious and didactic activities of the Jesuits, and was carried out under the supervision of Giovanni Tristani and, later, Francesco Costa and Alfio Vinci. The building, completed around the second half of the 16C, was a rare example of Renaissance elegance in an essen-

Bottom: Church of Casa Professa. Façade.

Church of Casa Professa. Central apse.

Church of Casa Professa. Detail of the "variegated marble" decoration.

Opposite page: Church of Casa Professa. Cupola (top) and high altar (bottom).

tially medieval environment. However, the affirmation of baroque taste and the need to enlarge the complex led to substantial renovation, which was begun in 1591 and completed in 1633 under the supervision of Father Natale Masucci (a Jesuit architect, who transformed the interior of the 16C building into the most sumptuous 17C church in Palermo). The present plan, with its nave, two aisles and deep side chapels, is the result of this renovation work. The façade, in late-16C style, has a linear layout and a sober decoration. Its sculptural ornamentation includes a notable 16C statue of the "Madonna della Grotta". The internal surfaces are entirely covered with marble inlays, depicting plant, human, animal and abstract motifs. This decorative masterpiece, which took two centuries to complete (until the end of the 18C), was the work of a host of artists, including Baldassare Pampilonia, Gioacchino Vitaliano, Pietro Nucifora and G. B. Ferreri.

The internal wall of the façade is characterized by an elegant layout and skilfully executed sculptural enamels which make it an 18C decorative masterpiece. In the lower part, to the left, two putti playing with a lion represent the uncontaminated human nature; to the right, two putti overwhelmed by a lion symbolize, on the contrary, the cor-

ruption of human nature. Above, two bas-reliefs depict Jesus healing a blind man (right) and Jesus and the Samaritan (left), notable works attributed to Vitaliano (1669-1739). On the pediment are two delicate sculptures depicting Jesus as a child and two Angels, by Marabitti. The interior houses two masterpieces by Pietro Novelli: San Filippo d'Argirò and St Paul the Hermit (1635). There is also a copy of Novelli's Annunciation, executed by the artist's daughter, Rosalia. In the Presbytery and Apse there are notable sculptures by Vitaliano. On the vault of St Anne's Chapel, entirely covered with lavish marble decoration, is a fresco attributed to Novelli. The chapel dedicated to St Ignatius was richly decorated at the beginning of the 17C. The statue of the Saint was sculptured in 1856 by Gian Maria Benzoni.

Church of Santa Maria di Valverde

The church stands in the square of the same name. Built in the 16C, it was enlarged by Mariano Smiriglio in 1633. The interior is sumptuously decorated with variegated marble and contains sculptures and paintings depicting various subjects. The marble ornamentation was executed by Paolo Amato and, later, by Andrea Palma; the 19C classical decoration of the apse is the work of G. Patricolo. Above the high altar is a Madonna del Carmelo by P. Novelli.

Church of San Domenico (the "Pantheon of the Sicilians")

The church, which stands in the square of the same name, was built in 1640 – a period when the Dominican Order was expanding and gaining prestige – to a design by the Dominican architect Andrea Cirrincione. It partly occupies the site of a 15C

Church of San Domenico. Façade.

Church of San Domenico. Angel in the Column of the Virgin.

Opposite page: Church of San Domenico. Nave (top) and funerary monument of Isidoro La Lumia (bottom).

church which, in turn, resulted from the restoration and enlargement of a 14C construction, the first building to be erected by the Dominicans on their arrival in Palermo in 1217. However, the only remains of these earlier constructions are three aisles of the adjoining cloister, which date from the 14C, while the fourth is coeval with the existing church. The façade and the internal decoration date from the 18C. Since the last century, the church has been the *Pantheon* of illustrious Sicilians. In fact, it contains numerous tombs, cenotaphs and memorial tablets. Among the most interesting works of art is a delicate sculpture depicting St Catherine, by Antonio Gagini, and Canova's female figure in the funerary monument of A. Turrisi Colonna. The funerary monument of G. Ramondetta, designed by P. Amato, also features sculptures by G. Serpotta. To the left of the church is the cloister and the former monastery. Some capitals in the cloister bear the coat of arms of the Chiaramonte family, who contributed to the construction of the earliest church. In the northern part are traces of the frescoes executed in 1526, which originally covered all the walls. The former monastery now houses the "Società Siciliana per la Storia Patria" (Sicilian Historical Society), established in the 19C to promote historical research on Sicilian civilisation. It houses a valuable library and a Museum of the Risorgimento, where numerous relics of the period are displayed.

Church of Sant'Anna

The church, situated in the square of the same name, was erected in the early 17C. The elegant and sinuous façade, however, was built in the 18C to a design by the architect Giovanni Amico. The two superimposed orders – characterized by perfect proportions – are different in size, the second order being limited to the width of the nave. The façade is embellished by vases, niches and statues executed by Giacomo Pennino and Lorenzo Marabitti from models and drawings by Giacomo Serpotta. In the interior is an 18C fresco depicting the Ascension, by Vito d'Anna.

Church of Sant'Anna. Façade.

Church of Sant'Anna. Sculptural ensemble in a niche of the façade.

Church of San Giuseppe dei Teatini

The church, situated on the south corner of Piazza Vigliena, was erected for the Theatine Fathers in 1645 but the internal decoration was completed in the 18C. Built to a design by the Theatine friar Giacomo Besio, it is the work of skilful artists, including Giuseppe Mariani who designed the splendid dome. The interior is covered entirely with precious marble, which creates a sumptuous and elegant effect. In the dome vault are frescoes by the Flemish painter Wilhelm Borremans. The frescoes on the nave vault, by Filippo Tancredi, were restored on the basis of photographic records. Above the imposing altar, designed by Andrea Palma and decorated with marble inlays, is a painting of San Gaetano by Pietro Novelli. Above the high altar is a notable work of popular art, a Crucifix by Fra Umile da Petralia. From the interior of the church, a staircase leads down to a large crypt, the Church of the Madonna della Provvidenza.

Church of San Giuseppe dei Teatini.
Top: Cupola and view of the nave.
Bottom: Decorative detail.

Church of San Matteo

The church, situated in Corso Vittorio Emanuele, not far from Piazza Vigliena, was built between 1633 and 1647 by the Confraternity of the Miseremini. The façade, designed by Carlo D'Aprile and Gaspare Guercio, is in three orders, unified by sumptuous volutes. The Latin-cross interior, with barrel vaults and an airy cupola, is rich in 18C decorations. The haut-reliefs above the door and the pillars – the four stucco statues representing Faith, Hope, Charity and Justice – are the work of Giacomo Serpotta. The church also houses paintings by Pietro Novelli and a Madonna attributed to Domenico Gagini. The vaults of the nave and of the cupola feature frescoes by Vito D'Anna, which are among the few remaining works of the greatest Palermitan fresco-painter.

Church of San Matteo, interior. Fresco in the vault depicting "The Triumph of the Souls in Purgatory" by Vito D'Anna (1754).

Triumphal Monument to King Philip V.

Monument to Philip V

This sculptural "ensemble", in front of the entrance to the Royal Palace, was executed in 1661 by Carlo D'Aprile, Vincenzo Guercio, Gaspare and Pietro Serpotta, and Luigi Geraci. It features allegorical statues of the eight States ruled by Philip IV (to whom the monument was originally dedicated). The four naked figures kneeling before Philip V represent the kings of Granada, Mauritania, the Caciques (America) and Mindanao (Asia).

Church of the Madonna della Pietà

The church, whose main front looks onto Via Torremuzza, was begun in 1678 to a design by Andrea Cirrincione and completed by Giacomo Amato between 1689 and 1723. The imposing façade, in two superimposed orders (Corinthian and Composite), is enlivened by the contrast between its marble and tufa parts. The statue of St Dominic above the main door is the work of Giacomo Vitaliano. In the interior, a spacious vestibule with a double row of columns leads into the single nave with short chapels. Stuccoes by Giuseppe, Giacomo and Procopio Serpotta decorate the vestibule and the church walls. In the vestibule, 21 panels contain frescoes depicting stories and miracles of St Catherine, by Wilhelm Borremans. In the vault of the presbytery is the fresco of the Triumph of Faith, by Gaspare Serenario.

Church of San Francesco Saverio

The church stands in the square of the same name, in the Albergheria quarter. It was built between 1685 and 1710 by the Jesuit architect Angelo Italia, and is particularly interesting because of its plan – a Greek cross with four hexagonal chapels at the corners – which is unique among Palermitan churches of the same period. The chapels, with a two-storey elevation, open onto the interior through an arcade created in the central area. This spatial arrangement is one of the most sumptuous reinterpretations of the Byzantine central-plan model, which was in vogue again in 16C Italy. The interior features a variegated marble ornamentation; a painting of St Calcedonio by Gaspare Serenario, in the first chapel to the left, and a painting of St Francis Xavier, probably the work of Girolamo Girardio, in the fourth chapel.

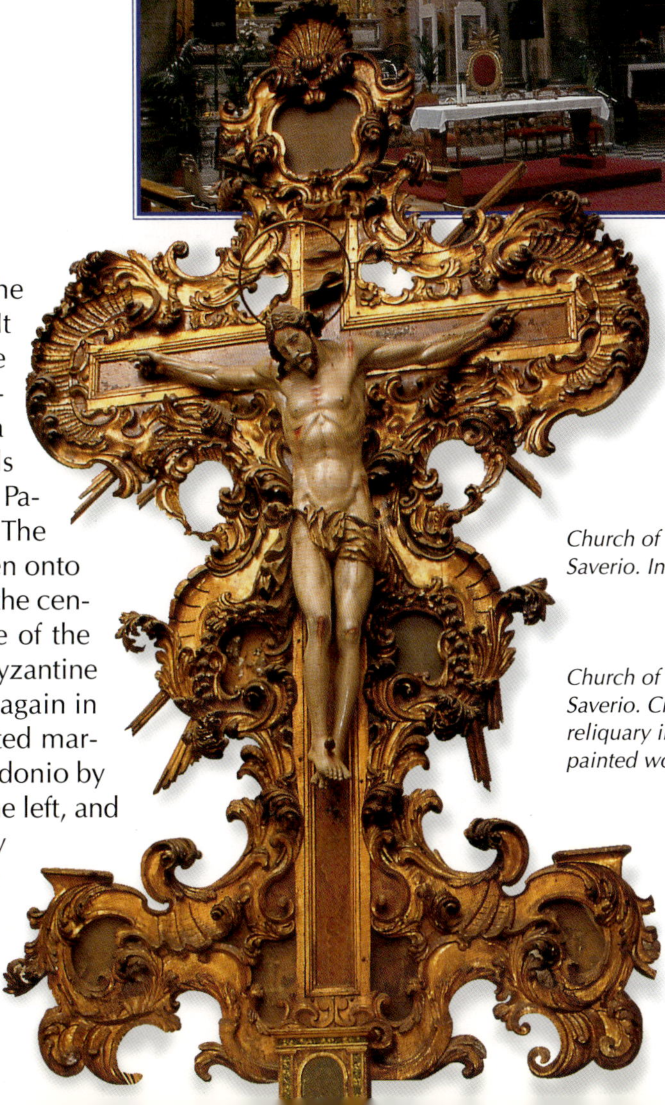

Church of San Francesco Saverio. Interior.

Church of San Francesco Saverio. Cross-shaped reliquary in carved and painted wood.

Fontana del Garraffo.

Fontana del Garraffo

The fountain, on the west corner of Piazza Marina, was built in 1698 to a design by Paolo Amato, an architect of the Palermitan Senate. It was originally conceived for another square, Piazza del Garraffo (in the *Vucciria* quarter), to replace a pre-existing fountain fed by an underlying spring. After about 120 years it was moved to its present position. The elegant architectural and sculptural ensemble reproduces some models of "movable machines" designed by Amato for processions and feasts.

Church of Santa Teresa alla Kalsa

Church of Santa Teresa. Façade and detail of the tondo depicting "The Holy Family", above the main entrance.

Situated in the square of the same name, the church was built at the end of the 17C to a design by the architect Giacomo Amato, for the nearby Carmelite nunnery. The monumental tufa façade is one of the most remarkable expressions of the Palermitan 17C. The interior is decorated with notable frescoes, some of which are probably the work of Gaspare Serenario and Vito D'Anna: four Biblical Stories on the walls and the Holy Family in the first chapel to the right. The stuccoes and the two statues of St Anne and St Therese in the apse are the work of Giuseppe and Procopio Serpotta.

Church of the Santissimo Salvatore

Situated in Corso Vittorio Emanuele, not far from Piazza Bologni, the church was built at the end of the 17C to a design by Paolo Amato, on the site of a pre-existing medieval church annexed to a Basilian convent. The building is polygonal in plan and is surmounted by a majestic dome, internally decorated with the Apotheosis of St Basil, a fresco by Vito D'Anna. After adequate restoration, it is now used as an *Auditorium*.

Oratory of San Lorenzo

The oratory stands in Via Immacolata and can be entered from Piazza San Francesco. It was built in the 16C by the Order of St Francis and is entirely decorated with Serpotta's stuccoes depicting stories of St Lawrence and St Francis. The altar was also executed by Serpotta to a design by Giacomo Amato.

Piazza Bologni and Palazzi Alliata, Ugo and Belmonte-Riso

Piazza Bologni. Bronze statue of Charles V; large coat of arms on Palazzo Alliata di Villafranca.

The square, also called Piazza d'Aragona in honour of Don Carlos of Aragon, who presided over the Kingdom from 1566 to 1567, was created in 1573. It was named Piazza Bologni after Don Aloisio Bologna, Baron of Montefranco, who built his palace there (the present-day Palazzo Alliata). In the 17C-18C the square became the "showcase" of the Palermitan aristocracy. In the middle is the bronze monument to Charles V (originally conceived for the Octagon of Piazza Vigliena), the work of Scipione Li Volsi. Palazzo Ugo, on the east corner of the square, behind the statue – its façade featuring two 16C marble statues of the Gaginesque school – still bears witness to the square's ancient splendour, together with Palazzo Alliata and Palazzo Belmonte-Riso. The former residence of the Bologna family, Palazzo Alliata (on the right side of the square) was restructured and restored by G. B. Vaccarini between 1664 and 1687. Palazzo Belmonte-Riso was built at the end of the 18C by the architect Venanzio Marvuglia, and after being almost completely destroyed by air bombing during the last World War has recently been restored.

Oratory of Santa Caterina

In the Olivella quarter (Via Monteleone) stands the 18C Oratory of Santa Caterina D'Alessandria, featuring stucco decorations and allegorical statues of the Sciences, by Giacomo and Procopio Serpotta. The Martyrdom of St Catherine, above the altar in the presbytery, is the work of Giuseppe Salerno, known as "lo Zoppo di Gangi".

Via Maqueda, Palazzo Santa Croce-Sant'Elia and Palazzo Comitini

Along Via Maqueda are several 17C-18C buildings but, for brevity's sake, only two of them will be described here. Palazzo Santa Croce-Sant'Elia (at no. 87) has wide windows crowned by pediments and wrought-iron balconies with the characteristic "goose-breast" profile, a recurrent motif in Sicilian architecture of the time. Palazzo Comitini, now housing the offices of the Province of Palermo, was built between 1766 and 1771 by the architect Nicolò Palma for the Princes of Comitini. The sumptuous halls of the piano nobile have rococo decorations by Gioacchino Martorana and panels from other 18C palaces, attributed to Elia Interguglielmi, a painter of the second half of the 18C.

Palazzo Gangi-Valguarnera

Palazzo Gangi-Valguarnera, the magnificent Mirror Room. The sumptuous interiors are highly evocative of the luxurious life led by Palermo's aristocracy during the last few centuries. The rooms of this palace provided the setting for the scenes of the Grand Ball in Luchino Visconti's film "The Leopard", based on the novel of the same name.

The palace stands in Piazza Croce dei Vespri, so called because here, in 1282, the Palermitans killed – and presumably buried – all the Angevins who had barricaded themselves in the palace of the Governor of Palermo, Jean de Saint-Rémy. In 1737, a column was erected to commemorate this episode (the existing one is a copy). The palace occupies a vast area. The front overlooking the square consists of the ground floor and piano nobile. The rear side, renovated around 1913 by Ernesto Basile, has a second floor extending as far as the internal courtyard and overlooking Piazza del Teatro Santa Cecilia. The internal staircase leads up to the piano nobile, consisting of a series of sumptuous and well-preserved rooms, whose walls are decorated and covered with damask of different colours. The vault of the ballroom is decorated with Serpotta-inspired stuccoes and frescoes by the painter Elia Intergugliemi. The ballroom leads into the rococo Mirror Room. In the vault is a fresco depicting Faith, by the painter Gaspare Serenario.

Villa Niscemi

Villa Niscemi. External view and a room.

Originally a large Baglio (ancient fortified farmhouse) equipped with a robust tower, the construction was extensively restored in the 18C. It stands in Piana dei Colli, where numerous aristocratic villas surrounded by vast gardens were constructed in the 18C. The present name of the villa derives from Prince Valguarnera of Niscemi, Peer of the Kingdom, who inherited it from Princes La Grua and Talamanca of Carini. The surrounding park has fortunately been preserved and the restored construction still retains all the original furnishings. It houses a collection of portraits of kings of Sicily and a library containing about 4,000 volumes. It is now the property of the Palermo Municipality, which bought it in 1987 to house its prestigious reception halls. From the villa there is a fine view of the nearby Palazzina Cinese (Chinese Palace) and of "The Leopard's" Villa, once the property of the Lampedusa family.

Villa Niscemi. Detail of a fresco.

Mummified bodies in the "Capuchin Catacombs".

Capuchin Catacombs

The Capuchin Monastery, built in the 17C on the site of a 16C construction, is situated at the end of Via Pindemonte. Beneath the restored church are the catacombs, vast spaces covered by vaults, which contain the mummified bodies of thousands of clergymen and people of all ranks who were buried there between the 17C and the early 19C. The state of preservation of many of the skeletons gives the place a suggestive – and almost macabre – atmosphere. Among those who were greatly impressed by the "catacombs" was the poet Ippolito Pindemonte.

Left: Mummified body of Friar Silvestro da Gubbio, the first to be buried in the catacombs on 16 October 1599.
Below: Mummified body of a young girl.

Fortresses, walls, bastions and urban gates

Evidence dating from as early as the Roman conquest indicates that only the upper and most ancient part of Panormos – the *Paleapolis* – was effectively fortified. The Romans extended and strengthened the ancient city walls. Traces of these fortifications can still be seen beneath the Church of San Cataldo and the complex of the ancient "military quarter" facing Corso Alberto Amedeo. In medieval times, Palermo became the capital of a vast Kingdom and expanded considerably, so that new boundary walls were necessary. These took a long time to build, and linked the city and the ancient Cala port in a unified urban complex. The medieval walls had numerous gates, but their precise number and names are still controversial. Of these, only Porta Sant'Agata and Porta Mazara (near the Children's Hospital) have remained, more or less intact, together with short stretches of walls. Thanks to these city walls, the Palermitans were able to defend themselves against the Angevin siege of 1325. Meanwhile, the *Castrum Superius* (the Royal Palace, now the seat of the Regional Government) was equipped with four high towers, of which only the "Pisana" (or Tower of St Ninfa) remains. The *Castrum Inferius* (the Castellammare) was given a regular four-sided layout, protected by walls.

18C constructions on the Papireto Bastion.

In the 15C, with the beginning of the viceroyal administration, the Castellammare was further fortified and became the second seat of the viceroys (the *Steri* had formerly been used). The ancient four-sided perimeter of the *Castrum* was surrounded by new walls, and the gateway to the city was equipped with two polygonal corner towers and a ravelin. Spared from the demolition work carried out in 1923-1924, this part of the Castellammare has been restored and is now visible, as is the 15C cylindrical tower on the west corner. This tower characterizes the entire south-west front of the fortress, which has recently been excavated and restored. During the first restructuring of the city walls, supervised by the royal architect Pietro Tomasello, a number of circular-plan bastions were added. Later, the architect Antonio Ferramolino ordered that the ancient walls should be completely rebuilt and fortified with bastions. Construction began in 1530 and continued to the end of the century. The external walls of the Castellammare were fortified with two bastions, and the vulnerable towers of the Royal Palace were shortened. The city walls were equipped with 13 bastions: San Giorgio, San Giuliano, San Vito, Aragona, Papireto, San Giacomo, Royal Palace, Gonzaga, Sant'Agata, Sant'Antonio, Spasimo, de Vega, del Tuono. Of these, only three have remained – the Spasimo, Royal Palace and Papireto Bastions. A few stretches of the walls are still visible, albeit half-hidden by buildings at certain points such as those behind Via Lincoln. The gates which have remained architecturally intact are: Porta Sant'Agata, Porta Mazara, Porta Nuova, Porta dei Greci, Porta Felice, Porta di Vicari, Porta Carini and Porta Reale Carolina. Between the 17C and 18C, the city's defence system was completed by small forts with low dykes, designed for opening fire on enemy ships with low topsides. These were: Forte della Lanterna, Forte della "Castelluccia" (near the North Dock) and Forte della Garita (on the South Dock). They were all demolished between 1848 and 1923 (the year when the Castellammare was also demolished). The

watchtowers built along the coast between the 16C and 17C completed the defence of the port. Some of these are still visible, such as the Arenella, Vergine Maria, Rotoli and Acqua dei Corsari towers.

City walls

One of the best-preserved sections of the fortified walls is the eastern front overlooking the Marina Promenade (or Foro Italico). The first stretch, which starts from Porta Felice, was laid out in 1823 as a "Public Terrace". It has maintained the name of Mura delle Cattive, which originally referred to the widows who used to walk there, to enjoy the pleasant air and the fine view of the gulf.

Castellammare Fortress

South-west Front – This part of the ancient fortress has recently been excavated and restored. It consists of a front of the city walls (reduced to half their height in 1922-1923) with the 15C entrance flanked by two towers, the "fixed" bridge over the ditch and the base of the ravelin. At the end of the walls is the sturdy circular bastion with embrasures and the underlying casemate covered by a cupola. The entire complex was built in the 15C, first under King Alfonso "the Magnanimous" and later under King Ferdinand "the Catholic".

Castellammare Fortress. The 15C entrance.

Porta Sant'Agata.
Engraving by A. Bova, from L. Triziano, "Le porte della città di Palermo al presente esistenti, ..." Palermo, 1732.

Bottom:
West side of the Porta Nuova.
Top, right:
Detail of the captive Moors.

The so-called "Torre Mastra" (Main Tower) – These suggestive architectural remains were not actually part of the Main Tower of the fortress; in fact, they are the precious vestiges of a corner of the *Palatium Vetus quod dicitur Maris Castellum* (as referred by medieval sources). They may be the ruins of the last residence of the Saracen governors of the city and first seat of Roger I of Hauteville, Great Count of Sicily (11C), prior to the construction of the Royal Palace by Roger II. The building was later rearranged by Frederick II, who added the scarp and sentry-boxes.

Porta Sant'Agata

The gate, which stands between Corso Tuköry and Via Cesare Battista, was part of the medieval walls and is almost certainly one of the most ancient gates in Palermo. To its side, along Via Cesare Battisti, are the ancient city walls, which have unfortunately been altered by the presence of shops hollowed out in the thick stonework.

Porta Felice. East side.

Porta Mazara

This gate, situated near the Children's Hospital in Piazza Porta Montalto, is coeval with Porta Sant'Agata but architecturally more complex. It was later incorporated into the Montalto Bastion. When this was demolished, the older structures of the gate were spared and brought to light again.

Porta Nuova

Porta Nuova (New Gate), located at the end of the Cassaro, was built in 1538 by the Palermitan Senate on the site of a less sumptuous gate, to celebrate the triumphal entry into Palermo of Emperor Charles V (1535), after his victorious military campaign against the Saracens in Tunis. Seriously damaged, in 1667, by an explosion of gun powder triggered by a flash of lightning, the gate was rebuilt in the same architectural form by Gaspare Guercio, architect of the Senate, with the addition of the upper loggia and pyramidal cusp covered with majolica tiles. The outer elevation, overlooking Piazza Indipendenza, features Mannerist elements, such as ashlars, grotesque figures, garlands and imposing Telamones representing captive Moors. On the inner elevation are four allegorical figures of Peace, Justice, Truth and Abundance.

Porta dei Greci. Engraving by A. Bova, from L. Triziano, "Le porte della città di Palermo al presente esistenti, ..." Palermo, 1732.

Porta dei Greci

The walls of the Foro Italico are interrupted by the archway of Porta dei Greci, built around 1553 in Mannerist style. Above the gate is Palazzo Forcella, erected in the 19C on the site of a building owned by the Prince of Cattolica and demolished during the political uprisings of 1820.

Porta Felice

The gate was named after Donna Felice Orsini, the wife of Viceroy Marcantonio Colonna, who ordered its construction. Work was commenced at the beginning of 1584 but was mostly carried out in the 17C. The lower level was built to a design by an unknown architect, whereas the upper level and the external decorations, completed in 1637, were supervised by three architects of the Senate: Mariano Smiriglio, Pietro Novelli and Vincenzo Tedeschi. The various phases of construction are reflected in the different styles which characterize the two levels: well-balanced the first, of Mannerist taste the second. The side overlooking the town is composite, with Mannerist features; the elevation overlooking the seafront is sumptuous and solemn.

Porta di Vicari (or di Sant'Antonino)

Situated at the end of Via Maqueda, overlooking the square of the same name, the present-day gate was built in the late 18C to replace a 17C gate erected after the opening of Via Maqueda, in a similar architectural form. At the sides are two 18C fountains.

Porta Carini

The present-day gate is an 18C reconstruction of a pre-existing one which dated from as early as the 14C. It is the entrance to the Capo market from Via Volturno.

Porta Real Carolina

This gate was named after Queen Maria Carolina, the wife of Ferdinand of Bourbon, and was the last to be erected (1786). At that time Villa Giulia, which attracted crowds of Palermitans on summer evenings, was outside the city walls. The Senate thus ordered the construction of this new gate, closer to the Villa, to make it easier to reach.

THE ARISTOCRATIC 19th CENTURY AND THE MIDDLE-CLASS 20th CENTURY

At the beginning of the 19C, the first urban plan was passed to extend the city outside its ancient boundaries, beyond the northern walls. Via Maqueda was extended as far as Piano di Santa Oliva, and Via Libertà was thus created (1848-49), a long avenue which was to connect the city centre with Piana dei Colli, marking a turning point in Palermo's urban development. Later, this also led to the demolition of a large part of the ancient city walls. As has already been mentioned, only a few stretches of the fortified walls and three bastions remain. In the early 19C, the seat of the University was established in the former Theatine House near the Quattro Canti. The 1860 war led to the end of the Kingdom of the Two Sicilies and to the annexation of Sicily to the Kingdom of Italy, ruled by the House of Savoy. Palermo and Sicily thus lost the little autonomy they had enjoyed during the Kingdom of the Two Sicilies. In 1866, the Kingdom of Italy introduced the so-called "subversive laws", which suppressed the ancient Confraternities, Arts and Crafts Associations and Charitable Institutions. As a consequence, the buildings which belonged to the Craftsmen and to the Congregations were confiscated, and the works of art they contained were dispersed. Some of the city's most famous architectural monuments began to decay; churches and oratories were transformed into barracks, courts, prefectures, State offices, or used as warehouses. Paintings, altars, church furnishings and *vare* (movable frames for carrying sacred images in procession) were brutally appropriated, sold or destroyed. The most ancient public festivals, such as the Festino (St Rosalia's festival) and the procession of the *cerei* (candles), were abolished. A large part of the population (the lower classes), which lived off the mutual aid system typical of the Confraternities, was reduced to poverty. This situation led to the tragic revolt known as "del 7 e mezzo" because for seven and a half days Palermo and its environs were in the hands of the rebels (September 1866). Later, to appease the population and give new impetus to the local economy, numerous public works were begun. In the meantime, the city began to see the spread of mass immigration as a last resort to escape from a situation which, for the poorer classes, had become unbearable.

Piazza Castelnuovo. Bronze sculpture of the Art of Navigation (by M. Rutelli, 1894).

The city also tried to react against the unhappy political situation caused by post-unity disappointment. In the 19C, the professional and entrepreneurial middle-class (including the Florio, Biondo and Ducrot families, Emanuele Notarbartolo, etc.) emerged and gained administrative and political power, replacing the land-owning aristocracy who, however, maintained their ancient prestige. Mayors Notarbartolo and Bonanno gave the city a new aspect, adding new facilities. Public gardens were laid out in Piazza Marina (Villa Garibaldi), Piano di Palazzo (Villa Bonanno) and Via Libertà (Giardino Inglese). The architect G. B. Filippo Basile designed the largest opera house in Italy, the Teatro Massimo (begun in 1875 and completed in 1897), while the engineer Giuseppe Damiani Almeyda designed the Politeama Garibaldi, built in 1874. Later, thanks to the work of Ernesto Basile, the son of Filippo, Palermo became the capital of the elegant *liberty* architecture. Among Basile's best-known works are the Villa Igiea Hotel, Villa Florio, the Florio Pavilion, Villa Deliella (no longer extant), Villa Basile, the Kursaal Biondo (mutilated), the seat of the Cassa di Risparmio. The best painter of the time was Francesco Lojacono, while Mario Rutelli was the most famous sculptor.

In the meantime, Palermo was expanding beyond its ancient walls, into the area previously used for the great National Exposition of 1891. The railway station was inau-

gurated in 1886 in the opposite part of the city. Unfortunately, this was also the period when ancient constructions and quarters in the old city centre were demolished to make way for new streets and buildings. The construction of Via Roma, between 1894 and 1924, partly destroyed two ancient Mandamenti (districts). The "middle-class" city thus began to take shape, enhanced by the construction of the Kursaal Biondo and Teatro Biondo. In the 1930s, the Policlinico (General University Hospital) and the pompous Palazzo delle Poste (General Post Office) were built. The port was equipped with piers for ocean liners and the naval station was built. During the Anglo-American bombings of 1943, houses, industries and port facilities were destroyed, and about sixty valuable architectural buildings were totally destroyed or seriously damaged.

On 15 May 1946, a decree granted regional autonomy to Sicily on the basis of a special Statute, and the Royal Palace became the seat of the Regional Assembly. In the 1950s, crowds of people from the neighbouring provinces arrived in Palermo, mostly attracted by the prospects of a job in the regional administration. This resulted in an enormous building expansion: Piana dei Colli was so densely covered with buildings that the parks of the 18C aristocratic villas disappeared. Many of the 19C and *liberty* palaces in Via Libertà were pulled down to make way for large, modern blocks of flats. By the 1970s, the renowned lemon groves of the Conca d'Oro had disappeared from the countryside around the city, to be replaced by new residential quarters. The port was rebuilt, and the Shipyard grew more efficient and became Palermo's largest industry. The city expanded, experiencing the typical problems of the great metropolises. In the 1970s, it had a population of 700,000. To cope with the increasing number of university students, a large University campus was built, partly on the site of the ancient Park of Villa d'Orleans. The problem of the "urban renewal" of the old city centre had to be faced. In fact, the restoration of the ancient part of the city has been under way for a few years now, but much remains to be done.

Via Libertà

The first stretch of this avenue was ordered by the revolutionary government of 1848 (which named it Viale della Libertà, i.e. Avenue of Liberty), while the rest was built by later administrations. From the very beginning, it was the most beautiful street in Palermo, especially when the stretch starting from Piazza Politeama was laid out with three separate lanes – the central one being the widest – embellished with flowerbeds and majestic plane trees and flanked by villas with parks. The avenue is now 2.5 km long and, together with Via Ruggero Settimo, Via Maqueda and Via Oreto, makes up a road axis of 6 km, running NW-SE, which divides the city into two equal parts.

The first stretch finishes at Piazza Antonio Mordini and Piazza Francesco Crispi (with a monument to the great statesman of Albanian origin, sculpted by Rutelli in 1905). In Piazza Crispi stands the Church of the Croci and the remains of the former convent school for poor girls, built at the end of the 17C. The façade, in neo-Gothic style, is the work of G. B. Filippo Basile. Opposite is the Excelsior Hotel, built for the National Exposition of 1891-92. Going further along Via Libertà, to the right is the Giardino Inglese (Villa F. Crispi), an "English-style" public garden with numerous ornamental plants. In the last few decades, most of the ancient villas which characterized the final stretch of Via Libertà were demolished and replaced by large buildings. These have substantially altered the pleasant aspect which had made it one of the most beautiful avenues in Europe. Via della Libertà finishes at Piazza Vittorio Veneto, a circus characterized by a monument known as "la Statua", dedicated to the fallen of the First World War, by the architect Ernesto Basile.

Teatro Massimo

The theatre was designed and built by G. B. Filippo Basile, but completed by his son Ernesto at the end of the 19C. Its construction was opposed by many – who criticized the choice of the site (two convents had to be demolished to make way for the new building) and argued that the theatre was excessively large for the city – but strongly supported by the then mayor Notarbartolo. Work was begun on 12 January 1874 and finished only in 1897, after various vicissitudes

Teatro Massimo. Façade looking onto Piazza Verdi. One of the greatest opera houses in the world, it is the masterpiece of the architect Giovan Battista Filippo Basile. His son, the architect Ernesto Basile, was to become one of the masters of European Liberty style.

which embittered the last years of life of the designer, who died in 1891. The plan submitted by Basile appealed so much to the architect Goffredo Semper – the greatest authority of the time on theatre design – that it won the international competition for the best design project for the opera house, held in 1864. On account of some of its architectural features, the Teatro Massimo outclasses the *Opéra* in Paris and the *Opernhaus* in Vienna, built in the same period. It has a seating capacity of 1,640; the stage, 38.50 m wide, with an average depth of 37 m (max 50 m), can contain 700 people. The dome has a reticulated metallic framework which rests on rollers designed for moving it according to temperature variations. The Teatro Massimo is the third largest theatre in Europe. The bronze statues flanking the external stairway represent Opera (by Mario Rutelli) and Tragedy (by Benedetto Civiletti). The vast auditorium has five tiers of boxes; the stage curtain depicts Roger II of Sicily parading on the day of his coronation, by Giuseppe Sciuti. Only recently has the theatre been restored and reopened to the public for the opera and concert seasons.

Teatro Massimo. The auditorium.

Teatro Politeama "Garibaldi"

The theatre stands in the square of the same name, which is divided into two by the junction of Viale della Libertà and Via Ruggero Settimo. On the opposite side of the square is the statue of Carlo Cottone, a patriot and statesman of the first half of the 19C; in the small garden is a neoclassical bandstand by Salvatore Valenti. The other side of the square features the statue of Ruggero Settimo and the Politeama Garibaldi, in neoclassical style, built in 1874 to a plan by the architect G. Damiani Almeyda. The rooms to the left of the theatre house the "Empedocle Restivo" Modern Art

Gallery, with notable 19C and 20C works by Italian (mainly Sicilian) artists. The entrance to the Gallery is in Via Turati.

Top:
Teatro Politeama G. Garibaldi.

Ernesto Basile's works (Villa Igiea; Villa Florio; Villa Basile; Cassa di Risparmio)

Between the end of the 19C and the beginning of the 20C, new urban and suburban residences were built for the aristocracy and the middle class. Most of these were erected along Viale della Libertà, Via Villafranca, Via Dante and Via Notarbartolo. A new social group was appearing, the middle class, whose aesthetic model was the *Art Nouveau* or *Liberty* style (Floral Style). The most representative designer of the period was Ernesto Basile. He was an architect, but also a designer of furnishings and useful items, and can been defined as the first modern architect in a rather provincial Italy. His name – and that of Ducrot, a furniture company based in Palermo – is associated with the success of the Palermitan *Liberty* at a national level (Ernesto Basile designed Montecitorio Palace, the seat of the Italian Parliament, in Rome;

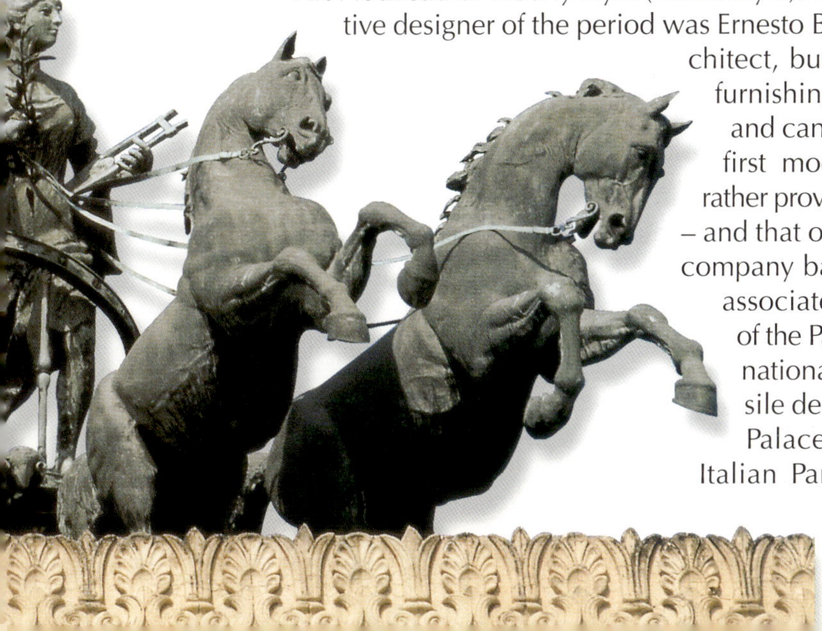

Bottom:
Detail of the bronze quadriga above the entrance portal (sculpted by M. Rutelli).

Hotel Villa Igiea (designed by the architect Ernesto Basile). Right: The banqueting hall. Below: External view.

Ducrot and other Palermitan companies supplied the furniture).

A host of architects, painters and decorators (Antonio Ugo, Mario Rutelli, Ettore de Maria Bergler) as well as skilful craftsmen (the heirs of a long-established tradition) followed this artistic current, contributing to Palermo's affirmation as one of the capitals of the *Liberty* style. The city offers an interesting itinerary which will allow the visitor to discover the most representative works of this fertile period. *Villa Igiea all'Acquasanta* was built in 1898, originally as a sanatorium, but was later transformed into a de-luxe hotel. The main hall, with a view of Villa Belmonte and Mount Pellegrino, is the part where the original furnishings have been best preserved. On the walls, around the woodwork designed by Basile, are the floral decorations executed by Ettore de Maria Bergler and his assistants. The overall architectural design of the building consists of an elegant series of pavilions, their forms skirting the outline of the enchanting stretch of rocky coast on which they were built. *Villa Florio all'Olivuzza* (1909) is one of Basile's finest, most dynamic and well-balanced works. *Villino Basile* (1904), in Via Siracusa, is among his most linear and modern creations, and was formerly the seat of the Superintendence of Monuments. Of the *Kursaal* and *Cinema Biondo* (1911) only the cinema, completely renovated, remains. The *Cassa di Risparmio* (1909-1912), which incorporated part of the former Monastery of the Mercedari Scalzi (Via Cartari), was the only building of the "public" sector to be erected in Palermo. Its external formalism, in keeping with the taste of the time, is also charac-

Top, left:
Palazzina Basile in Via Siracusa. Corner balcony.

Top, right:
Morello's Bakery (Capo quarter). Mosaic sign in Liberty style.

Bottom:
Kursaal Biondo.
Façade of the cinema-theatre.

terized by a severe elegance which enhances its noble aspect. However, these are only a few examples of Ernesto Basile's numerous and varied works, many of which have unfortunately been demolished. He renovated Palermo's appearance between the 19C and 20C also with his minor works, including the *Church of Santa Rosalia*, the *Florio Pavilion alla Colonnella* (in the Romagnolo quarter) and the *Kiosk* at the corner of Via Ruggero Settimo and Piazza Castelnuovo. Basile's followers (G. Benfratello, F. La Porta, V. Alagna, Caronia Roberti), albeit lacking his original and refined creativeness, were able to form a school of great formal elegance.

PALERMO'S FRAGRANT AND LUXURIANT GARDENS

As early as the Middle Ages, Palermo had several parks and gardens, the most famous and largest of which was the Park of the Kings of Sicily, which extended from the Royal Palace to the surrounding mountains. Traces of this Park can still be seen today, i.e. the buildings erected within its boundaries as royal pleasure residences

Villa Giulia. Fountain of the Genius of Palermo. Top: Romantically arranged ruins.

(Maredolce, Favara, Parco, Minnermo) and *Solatia* such as the Zisa, Cuba Soprana and Cuba Sottana. From the 14C onwards, the Park was divided into various estates belonging to the great Ministers of the Kingdom, Palermitan feudal lords and ecclesiastical authorities. Originally intended as a place for hunting, stock-farming, growing diversified crops and relaxation, the Park was later planted with citrus trees, especially lemons, whose colour accounts for the name given to the valley: Conca d'Oro (Golden Valley). Of this ancient and vast Park, only some of the *Solatia*, the ruins of other constructions surrounded by modern buildings and, here and there, a few lemon orchards have remained. There used to be numerous private gardens also within the city boundaries, but none of them have remained: for defensive reasons, in fact, the city withdrew into itself and every little scrap of space available was covered with buildings. In the 18C,

the city's Senate allowed the creation of a few private gardens in the grounds of the bastions.

Villa Giulia (or "Flora")

This garden, laid out by Nicola Palma in 1778, was located outside the city walls, near the de Vega Bastion. Called after Donna Giulia, the wife of Viceroy Guevara, it was perhaps the first public garden in Italy, and was deeply admired

Bottom: Botanical Garden. Fountain of Parides.

by J. W. Goethe during his stay in Palermo. In 1872 it was enlarged and embellished. Four neoclassical exedrae, designed by G. Damiani Almeyda, were created in the central plaza. These surround a fountain which features a putto bearing a twelve-sided marble figure with sundials (by Lorenzo Federici). The entrance from the Foro Italico is characterized by a monumental portal flanked by two marble lions.

Botanical Garden

Botanical Garden.
The "Gymnasium"
and a papyrus plantation.

An earlier Botanical Garden was established in the grounds of the Aragona Bastion in 1779. Ten years later, the structure was moved outside the city walls, in front of the Spasimo Bastion and adjacent to Villa Giulia, where it can still be admired today. The complex is characterized by the "Gymnasium", designed by the French architect Léon Dufourny. This is a square-plan building with Doric tetrastyle pronaoi (in two fronts) and an elegant dome. To its sides are the Calidarium and Tepidarium, designed by Venanzio Marvuglia in 1789, which house the herbaria. The vast garden (10 hectares) contains a very wide range of plant species from all over the world and is one of the most important botanical gardens in Europe.

"La Favorita" Park

In 1799, during his stay in Palermo, King Ferdinand of Bourbon (IV of Naples and III of Sicily) created this park – a magnificent complex of farmland, woods, residences and gardens – which has come down to us almost intact. King Ferdinand later set out a royal hunting estate in the wood known as Bosco della Ficuzza, near Corleone, where he also built a magnificent Royal Palace. The Favorita Park is characterized by the architectural complex of the Palazzina Cinese (Chinese Palace), with the adjoining buildings which house the G. Pitrè Ethnographic Museum. The Park is entered from Porta dei Leoni, the gate standing in the square of the same name. Then you go along Viale di Diana and Viale d'Ercole, 2.3 km long and flanked by beautiful holm-oaks. At the end of Viale d'Ercole is the majestic Fountain of Hercules. The Palazzina Cinese was built in 1799 to a project by G. Venanzio Marvuglia, in a peculiar style which is reminiscent of the *chinoiseries* in fashion at the time. It was the leisure residence of King Ferdinand and his wife Maria Carolina. The interiors are richly decorated in various styles. An ingenious mechanical device in the basement enabled the dishes to be served upstairs without the intrusion of servants into the rooms. The Palazzina Cinese overlooks a pleasant Italian-style garden, aligned with the building and now open to the public; the Città dei Ragazzi (a leisure centre for children) has recently been created in the area behind the Palace.

Opposite page:
La Favorita Park. Interior of the Palazzina Cinese.

Top: Palazzina Cinese.

Bottom: Villa D'Orleans Park, not far from the Royal Palace.

Villa d'Orleans

Going from Porta Nuova towards Corso Calatafimi, on the left you find Piazza Indipendenza (the former Piano di Santa Teresa, from the church of the same name). On the south side of the square stands Palazzo d'Orleans, the seat of the offices of the President of the Sicilian Region, with the magnificent garden laid out in 1797 as an agricultural experimental station. The site of the original park is now partly occupied by the buildings of some university faculties, in particular the Faculty of Agricultural Science which carries out its experiments here; the remaining area is used as a public garden.

Giardino Inglese (Via Libertà) and Giardino Garibaldi (Piazza Marina)

View of the Giardino Inglese.

To the right of Via Libertà, going northwards from Piazza Croci, is the Giardino Inglese, an English-style public garden with numerous ornamental plants and some plastic art

works, including a marble statue dedicated to the Canaris brothers, two heroes of Greek independence (by Civiletti, 1878). Behind the garden is the magnificent Villa Chiaramonte-Bordonaro (the work of E. Basile) with a fine park.

At the end of the 19C, a public garden (Giardino Garibaldi) was laid out in the middle of Piazza Marina – in the old city centre, below Palazzo Steri – on the initiative of the then mayor Notarbartolo. The garden was planted with rare exotic species, including an impressive *Ficus magnolioides* and a *Ficus citrifolia*. The iron railings, designed by G. B. F. Basile, are particularly elegant.

Giardino Garibaldi in Piazza Marina. Detail of a "Ficus magnolioides".

Bottom: Villa Bonanno.

Villa Bonanno

This public garden, named after Mayor Bonanno, was laid out in 1905 in the wide open space in front of the Royal Palace. One of the 12 grain storage pits built at the end of the 16C by the Palermitan Senate is still visible here, as are the interesting traces of the floor of one of the three Roman patrician villas (probably dating from the 1C AD) which once stood in the area. The site was originally used as a drill ground by the garrison which, until the 19C, was quartered in the Royal Palace and in the buildings on the north side of the square; the area was then planted with palms and transformed into a public garden.

MUSEUMS

"Antonio Salinas" Regional Archaeological Museum

The museum, housed in the former Monastery of the Congregation of St Philip and with its main entrance in Piazza dell'Olivella, is one of the foremost archaeological museums in Europe. The building, which was restored after being damaged during the

Archaeological Museum. Entrance courtyard. Fountain of Triton (16C).

Lèkythos depicting a "Departing warrior", by a painter from Haimon, 500-475 BC.

Second World War, contains archaeological items from various collections. The University Museum collection was acquired first. Then the metopes from Temple C of Selinunte and the finds collected by the Sicilian Commission for Antiques and Fine Arts were added, followed by the metopes of Temple E of Selinunte, finds from Solunto, Roman sculptures from Tindari, donations by the Bourbon sovereigns, the Gandolfo coin collection from Termini Imerese and many other items. After 1860, the museum collection was enriched by new acquisitions, including material confiscated from the clergy (1866) and, most importantly, the Bonci-Casuccini collection, the greatest collection of Etruscan art existing outside Tuscany.

In the smaller cloister on the ground floor, the following items are of particular interest: the famous "Palermo Stone" (instrumental in establishing the chronology of the most ancient Pharaohs) in the Egyptian collection, and two impressive anthropoid sarcophagi from Pizzo Cannita in the Phoenician-Punic collection. Along the walls of the larger cloister are epigraphs, architectural fragments and statues, and the colossal statue of Zeus enthroned (2C BC) from Solunto. The cloister leads into a small room with stelae from the *Zeus Meilichios* Sanctuary near Selinunte. The Pirro Marconi Room houses the lateral sima of the Temple of Victory at Himera (erected after the victory over the Carthaginians in 480 BC). In the adjacent room are four beautiful "Salinas" metopes (depicting the Delphic Triad, the Sphinx, the Rape of Europa and Hercules fighting the Bull) and two recently discovered metopes (Deity riding a Chariot; Offerings to the Goddesses). This is the highest aesthetic expression of the archaic and classical Siceliot culture. On the left are marble lamps in the form of female heads and reconstructions of part of the trabeations of the *Pronaos* from Temples C and F, with metopes of great historical and aesthetic value. Three metopes from Temple C depict Apollo's Chariot, Perseus and the Gorgon, Hercules and the Cercopes. The lower parts of two metopes from Temple F depict Dionysus killing a Giant and Athena against Enceladus. On the wall at the far end is the reconstruction of part of the frieze of the *Pronaos* from Temple E (470-460 BC) with some metopes (Hercules and the Amazon, the Marriage of Zeus, Artemis and Actaeon, Athena and Enceladus). The next rooms house the Casuccini Collection, the richest and most significant collection of Etruscan material from Chiusi existing outside Tuscany. Most of the items are sepulchral pillars (530-480 BC), including a funerary statue of the canopic type (5C BC). The second room houses archaic, classical and Hellenistic sculptures. In the third room is the sarcophagus of *Hasti Afurnei* (2C BC), while the fourth room houses a great canopic statue (6C BC) and a vast collection of "buccheri" (pottery) in-

Archaeological Museum.
Top:
Basalt statue (Isis?) from Campania, formerly in the Favorita Park (2C BC).

Bottom:
Bronze youth from Selinunte (Siceliot work, 480 BC).

cluding the famous *oinochoe* depicting the Myth of Perseus.

The visit continues on the first floor. In the northern gallery is a topographic section with material from different archaeological sites. The Terracotta Room includes finds from different collections. The Bronze Room displays Etruscan, Greek and Roman bronzes, including two very valuable works: Hercules killing the Ceryneian Hind (from Pompeii), a Roman copy of an original by Lysippus, and the Ram from Castel Maniace (Syracuse), a splendid Hellenic masterpiece (3C BC). The Greek Sculpture Room houses a fragment of the east front of the Parthenon frieze and a marble reproduction of a Satyr pouring a drink, by Praxiteles. The Roman Sculpture Room displays a fine Portrait of an Unknown Man (2C AD) from Partinico and, on the floor, the reconstruction of a mosaic floor with the Seasons, from Lilybaeum (3C AD).

Archaeological Museum. Statue of a young priestess of Isis, from Taormina (2C AD).

The second floor houses a collection of prehistoric finds from western Sicily, including a mould of the rock engravings in the Addaura Cave. Most of the items belong to the Aeneolithic cultures. The collection includes engraved pottery items in the Moarda style, dating from the Bronze Age. The Castelluccio pottery from Naro and Partanna is particularly interesting. There is also an outstanding Greek pottery collection (Corinthian, Ionic, Laconian, Attic, Etruscan and Italiot). The splendid items are decorated with famous Greek mythological figures (black figures on a clay background, or red figures on a black background). The vases are *deinos, oinochoe, lekane, lèkythos, epinetra* and *kylikes*, many of which bear the signature of their makers: Amasis, Douris, Andokides, Skythes, Oltos. A collection of Apulian, Campanian and Siceliot pottery follows (4C and 3C BC). There are also the reconstructions of three Roman mosaic floors discovered between 1868 and 1915 in Piazza Vittoria (Palermo), depicting the Triumph of Neptune, Orpheus and the animals, and a Dionysiac Ritual.

Archaeological Museum. Bronze ram (3C BC) from Syracuse. Together with its pair, it once decorated the portal of Castel Maniace in Syracuse and was later moved to the Royal Palace in Palermo.

Regional Gallery. The room with the two great hanging Crucifixes.

Regional Gallery. Statue of Madonna and Child, a splendid example of the elegance and grace which characterize the Madonnas sculpted by Antonello Gagini (1478-1536).

Sicilian Regional Gallery at Palazzo Abatellis

The museum is housed in the splendid 15C Palazzo Abatellis, in the old city centre between Piazza Marina and the Foro Italico, and can be entered from Via Alloro no. 1 (Kalsa quarter). The palace has been described in a previous chapter of this guide. The National (now Regional) Gallery was established in 1953-54, after adequate restoration of the building, which was damaged by bombing during the last World War. The museum has been designed to illustrate the development of figurative arts (painting, sculpture, applied arts, etc.) in Sicily from the 12C to the 18C. The works of art displayed mostly derive from donations, acquisitions and confiscations following the suppression of the religious orders in 1866. They were formerly part of the Royal University Picture Gallery and were later moved to the National Museum. The Regional Gallery contains 200 works of art, including priceless European masterpieces.

The first rooms contain medieval wooden carvings, 14C-15C sculptures and the 15C fresco depicting the *Triumph of Death* (formerly in Palazzo Sclafani), a sublime synthesis of European pre-Renaissance figurative art and a fascinating and disquieting

Regional Gallery.
The "Annunciation"
(1473) by Antonello da
Messina (1430-1479).

representation of the religious atmosphere of the time. There are also 16C sculptures and painted panels from wooden ceilings. On the first floor is the picture gallery, with paintings from the 13C to the 16C, including the famous *Annunciation* by Antonello da Messina. Later works include a marble statue of the *Madonna del Latte*, by Domenico Gagini; the fresco of the *Holy Virgins* by Tommaso de Vigilia; the outstanding marble bust of a Lady, perhaps depicting Eleanor of Aragon, by Francesco Laurana, and the refined *Malvagna Triptych*, by the Flemish painter Jean Gossaert, known as Mabuse (16C). Other 16C works are the *Flight into Egypt* by Vincenzo de Pavia; *St Peter and St Paul* by Riccardo Quartararo, and the marble *Madonna del Riposo* by Antonello Gagini.

Regional Gallery. Fresco of the"Triumph of Death", formerly in Palazzo Sclafani (anon., 15C).

Regional Gallery.
Top: The "Malvagna Triptych", depicting the Madonna enthroned with the Holy Child, by the Flemish painter Jean Gossaert, known as Mabuse (16C).

Bottom: The famous "Bust of Eleanor of Aragon" by Francesco Laurana, a sculptor and medallist from Zara (1425-1502).

The collection includes several works by Flemish painters who were active in Sicily in the 16C: Jan Provost, Adriaen Ysenbrant, Jan Van Scorel, Simone De Wobreck. The 17C and 18C are gloriously represented by the *Madonna and Child with St John the Baptist and St Rosalia*, by Pietro Novelli; the *Return of Joseph's brothers* by Francesco Solimena and other works by Corrado Giaquinto, the Cavaliere d'Arpino, Bartolomeo Cavarozzi, Francesco Albani and Mattia Preti.

Diocesan Museum

The museum, housed in the Archbishop's Palace, was founded in 1927 by Cardinal Alessandro Lualdi in accordance with the directives sent by Pope Pious XI to all the dioceses. It contains paintings, sculptures, church furnishings and vestments, all items of great artistic and historical value dating from the 13C-16C. The paintings include small Byzantinesque panels, altar-pieces, diptychs and triptychs which seem to combine the strong Byzantine tradition and the new Latin influences which spread through Sicily between the 14C and 15C. The main themes are those connected with the exaltation of the Madonna. Most of the works are by unknown authors; their formal adherence to the styles of central Italy and Sicily is offset by the graceful expression and posture of the figures and by their fabulous golden backgrounds or poetic starry skies. Subtle Spanish and Flemish influences, as well as Tuscan Renaissance features, are present in the 15C and 16C works. After a series of anonymous works, the first recognizable authors appear: Tommaso De Vigilia (15C); Pietro Ruzzolone (first half of the 16C); Riccardo Quartararo; Mario di Laurito (the author of an outstanding panelled wooden ceiling, in the Church of the Annunziata); Vincenzo Da Pavia; Giuseppe Sirena; Vincenzo La Barbera; Pietro D'Asaro. Numerous Flemish painters were active in Sicily in this period. The museum displays paintings by Simone De Wobreck, while the museum chapel is decorated with frescoes by Wilhelm Borremans.

Diocesan Museum.
Mario Di Laurito,
"Madonna and Saints",
tempera on wood, 1530.
The lower part of the painting depicts the city of Palermo.

The museum also houses an interesting collection of sculptures in marble and wood, mostly from the Gaginesque school which prevailed in Sicily between the end of the 15C and the beginning of the 16C. Some of these, especially the decorative sculptures, were part of the famous marble Retablo by Antonello Gagini, sculpted in 1507 for the Cathedral and unfortunately dismantled at the end of the 18C. The church furnishings and vestments displayed include skilfully executed processional crucifixes, chalices, reliquaries, ostensories, ciboria, chasubles, copes, tunicles, stoles, etc.

The collections of the "Fondazione Mormino del Banco di Sicilia"

These valuable collections are housed in a building in Via Libertà. The "Foundation for the Cultural and Economic Development of Sicily" was established in 1923. In 1954 it was named the "Ignazio Mormino Foundation for the Economic, Cultural and Touristic Development of Sicily" in honour of the general manager of the Banco di Sicilia (Bank of Sicily) who promoted its creation. This institution is now represented in the secretariat of the Bank. The Foundation has financed archaeological excavation campaigns, scientific collections and essays edited by experts in various fields, and has been awarded a gold medal by the Ministry of Education for its cultural, scientific and artistic merits. The rooms of the Foundation Museum house finds and items from a number of collections. The archaeological collection includes items of great scientific interest and notable aesthetic value from the excavations carried out at Solunto, Terravecchia di Cuti, Himera, Selinunte and Manicalunga. The majolica collection displays more than a hundred items, mostly of Sicilian craftsmanship and dating from different periods. There is also a display of Sicilian medieval and modern coins (from 1282 to 1836), together with a number of medals. The stamp collection features precious stamps issued by the Kingdom of the Two Sicilies in 1858-59. There is also

Exhibition room at the "Empedocle Restivo" Modern Art Gallery.

a collection of more than a thousand engravings, xylographs, etchings, black-and-white and colour lithographs, drawings, watercolours and temperas concerning various aspects of Sicily: topography, chorography, monuments, town planning, social customs and geography. The graphic collection includes works dating from the 17C-19C. There is a specialized library containing works about all the collections.

"Empedocle Restivo" Modern Art Gallery

The Gallery, housed in the Teatro Politeama, was established by Empedocle Restivo in 1906 and inaugurated in 1910. The collection consists of donations from private citizens and acquisitions by the city's Administration. It includes paintings and sculptures dating from the early 19C and 20C, mainly by Sicilian artists, and historical archives. Most of the 19C paintings are by artists of limited local renown, but there are also works by great painters such as Francesco Lo Jacono, the author of vast and airy landscapes with deep backgrounds, Antonino Leto, influenced by the "Neapolitan manner", Rocco Lentini, Ettore De Maria Bergler and many others. There are also works by non-Sicilian artists from the late 19C-early 20C, including D. Morelli, G. Toma, A. Mancini, G. Lega, G. Ciardi, G. Favaretto, G. Boldini, etc. The 20C is represented by the works of A. Terza, F. Carena, M. Sironi, F. Casorati, M. Campigli, C. Cagli, F. Pirandello, C. Carrà, A. Tosi, P. Rizzo and R. Guttuso. The Gallery houses a few sculptures, the most notable being those by Valerio Villareale, Benedetto Civiletti, Domenico Trentacoste, Ettore Ximenes and Mario Rutelli, the most talented sculptor, who was mainly active in Rome.

Ethnographic Museum. Ceremonial dress of a confraternity.

"Giuseppe Pitrè" Sicilian Ethnograhic Museum

This is one of the most famous ethnographic museums in Italy. It is the property of the Palermo Municipality and was created in 1909 by the great ethnographer Giuseppe Pitrè, the founder of the Italian school of folk psychology. Since 1935 the museum has been housed in the pavilions adjoining the Palazzina Cinese, in the Favorita Park. It displays the largest existing collection of items related to Sicilian "popular" life and culture, providing the most comprehensive documentation of the usages, customs, beliefs, myths, habits and traditions of the Sicilian people. The museum collections contain about 4,000 items, including 1,500 which were part of Pitrè's original collection, items from the ethnographic collections of the former Palermo National Museum, and others donated by private citizens. The items are displayed in 30 rooms, divided into 15 sections which have essentially maintained the layout designed by Giuseppe Cocchiara, a distinguished scientist and disciple of Pitrè.

The first section is dedicated to rural and urban dwelling places, from straw huts to the house of the *burgisi* (members of the middle class). The following sections are related to hunting and fishing, agriculture and sheep-farming, costumes, carvings and pieces of pottery, magic and religion, toys, feasts and shows, carts. A puppet theatre has been set up in one room, with various puppets (Angelica, Orlando, Morgante, Rinaldo) and posters depicting the scenes which the *Pupara* (puppeteers) represent on the stage. Then there

is the room dedicated to the Sicilian cart, with models showing the different stages of production, and the Christmas crib room, including works by unknown artists and by Giovanni Matera (a famous 18C potter). More than 300 statuettes represent the Nativity and the Slaughter of the Innocents. Other interesting rooms contain the coaches of the ancient Palermitan Senate, and models, drawings and prints of the most notable Triumphal Chariots of St Rosalia created in the 19C-20C. There is also a fine collection of *ex-votos*, including paintings on wood, tinplate and canvas, all depicting the miracle experienced by the donor in the naif traits of popular art. The museum also houses a specialized Library of about 30,000 volumes, including some valuable 16C books, numerous "popular" libretti, 1,500 degree theses, Giuseppe Pitrè's manuscripts, and letters written by various Italian and foreign scholars who corresponded with him. The Library also contains a notable collection of prints, engravings, small sacred images and photographs including an interesting series related to 19C Sicilian bandits and images of ancient Palermo.

Ethnographic Museum. Top: The annexe to the Palazzina Cinese (La Favorita Park) which houses the Museum.

Middle: Carriage.

Bottom: Marionette of the Puppet Theatre.

"Antonio Pasqualino" International Museum of Puppetry

This is one of the most fascinating puppet museums in Europe. It is situated in Via Butera no. 1, near Corso Vittorio Emanuele, and is dedicated to the scholar who promoted its creation. Established in 1975 by Palermo's Association for the Preservation of Popular Traditions, it houses more than 3,000 items. These include Sicilian "pupi" (string puppets), Neapolitan puppets, marionettes and puppets from all over Europe – some of which designed by famous modern painters (Guttuso, Baj, Kantor) –, Greek and Turkish "shadow puppets", African marionettes from Mali and Congo, and further items from China, Burma, the New Hebrides, Rajasthan, India, Southern Asia, Bali, Java, Thailand and Cambodia. The Museum also houses a specialized library and sound and film archives. The Association promotes a number of didactic activities and organizes exhibitions and performances, including the famous Morgana Festival which attracts puppet theatres from all over the world.

Museum of the Risorgimento. Portrait of Giuseppe Garibaldi (by Salvatore Li Greci).

Palazzo Mirto Museum

Situated between Via Merlo and Via Lungarini, near Piazza Marina, Palazzo Mirto was the residence of the Princes Lanza Filangeri, one of the most important families of the Sicilian aristocracy. It was donated to the Sicilian Region in 1982, on the understanding that its original furniture would be kept and that it would be opened to the public. The Regional Administration has converted the palace into a museum, and the interiors have been arranged by the Superintendence of the Cultural and Environmental Heritage of Palermo. The building has undergone substantial alterations over the centuries. Although it is not particularly interesting from an architectural point of view, its interiors are well worth a visit. The rooms, in fact, have maintained the typical furnishings of Palermitan aristocratic palaces, and reflect the evolution of aesthetic taste from the 18C to the early 20C. They conjure up the atmosphere and lifestyle of the period, which was both austere and sumptuous. The rooms contain furnishings and fittings, precious objects from different periods (mainly from the 18C-19C), frescoes, paintings, embroidered tapestry, canopies, "Chinese" parlours, oriental and Meissen porcelain, Murano glass chandeliers, tortoiseshell caskets, chinaware, glassware, Imari and Chinese vases, collections of 18C fans and other precious objects.

Museum of the Risorgimento

The Museum is run by the "Società Siciliana per la Storia Patria" (Sicilian Historical Society), housed in the former monastery of San Domenico, which can be entered from the square of the same name. The cultural institution was founded in 1873 to promote historical studies on Sicily. The Museum is on the ground floor of the building and contains exhibits mostly related to the 1860 revolution.

Palazzo Mirto Museum. A room. Frescoes, stuccoes, crystals, elegant and precious furniture, all contribute to conjure up the atmosphere of bygone times, when the members of Palermo's aristocracy seemed "akin to Gods"...

Other Museums

Other interesting museums in Palermo include the "G. G. Gemmellaro" Geological Museum in Corso Tuköry no. 131, and the "P. Piraino" Toy Museum in Via Bandiera no. 99. There are also numerous small museums in the vicinity of Palermo, such as the Modern Art Museum of Villa Cattolica in Bagheria, the Archaeological Museums (*Antiquaria*) of Himera and Solunto, the Civic Archaeological Museum of Marineo, the Archaeological and Ethnological Museum of Partinico, the Archaeological and Ethno-Anthropological Museum of San Cipirello, the "Baldassare Romano" Civic Museum of Termini Imerese, the *Antiquarium* Museum and the Permanent Exhibition of Sicilian Carts in Terrasini, and the "Nicola Barbato" Museum of Piana degli Albanesi.

FESTIVALS AND FOLKLORE

Palermo Diocesan Museum. Vincenzo La Barbera, "St Rosalia interceding for Palermo", oil on canvas, 1624.

The Triumphal Chariot of St Rosalia is the most distinctive element of the so-called "Festino", the great annual festival held in Palermo (13-15 July) in honour of Rosalia Sinibaldi, who miraculously freed the city from the terrible plague epidemic of 1624. Rosalia was a Palermitan girl of noble descent, who lived during the reign of King William I. She abandoned her father's house to live as a hermit in a cave on Mount Pellegrino, and was proclaimed saint after her death. During the plague of 1624, the Palermitans prayed for her heavenly intervention. Her bones were found in the cave where she had lived; they were brought to the city, put in a splendid silver urn and carried in procession. The plague epidemic ended and Rosalia was proclaimed patron saint of the city. It was decided that this miraculous event should be celebrated with a great annual festival, the Festino. Since then, the main elements of the festival have been the processions of the urn and of the Triumphal Chariot.

The silver urn containing the remains of St Rosalia is carried in procession through the streets of the old city centre, in the presence of the Bishop of Palermo, the city's authorities and the Confraternities. In former times, all the religious Orders, the Confraternities and the Arts and Crafts Associations of the city participated with their *vare* (movable frames for carrying sacred images in procession). The first Triumphal Chariot was created in 1686 for the 62nd edition of the Festino. This was mainly characterized by the presence of an orchestra and by the majestic proportions of the "machine", i.e. the Chariot. A Chariot similar in design but reflecting the evolution of taste over the various decades was built every year until 1859. The design of the Triumphal Chariot, of the "firework display machines" and of the external decoration of the most important buildings was entrusted to the most renowned architects of the time and to the architects of the Senate.

In the earliest editions of the Festino – between the 17C and 18C – the Chariot was mounted in Piano di Santo Spirito, where the restored fountain of the Sea Horse now stands. On 10 July it was yoked to about thirty pairs of oxen in front of Porta Felice, and drawn through the Cassaro. In the same period, it was preceded by quadrilles of small carts. Although many variants existed, the architectural structure of the Triumphal Chariot followed two fundamental mod-

Festino of St Rosalia.
Drummers.

els: the "ship" model, which was adopted throughout the 18C, and the vertical "candle" model, used in the 19C. In the 18C, the Chariot was gradually made higher and longer, and increasingly resembled a huge bugle studded with festoons, putti, allegorical figures and flying angels. The front part became thinner or arched, and supported sculptural groups, as in the Chariot designed by Andrea Palma in 1725. In 1765, for the first time, the Chariot was lit by torches, and carried through Via Toledo by night. The traditional night procession of the "*Carro addumatu*" (illuminated Chariot) thus began.

In the 19C, the "ship" model was gradually replaced by the "candle" model, with a more vertical design.

Triumphal Chariot of St Rosalia designed by Paolo Amato for the Festino of 1701.

Neoclassical decoration made the exterior of the "machine" seem colder, in spite of the polychrome tints which replaced the former monochrome painting, the most frequently used being gold. 19C Chariots measured as high as about 30 metres, but they appeared top-heavy, and not very elegant. After 1858, the construction of the Chariot was interrupted for the first time due to the start of levelling work in the Cassaro. However, it was resumed in the 1890s, in forms which imitated those of the beginning of the century. The same design was maintained in the first "recovery" of the Chariot by Giuseppe Pitrè, who reproduced the 1857 model. The Chariot was excluded again from the Festino of 1898, mainly due to the presence of tram wires, cables and lamps for public lighting above the city's streets, which would have made the procession difficult. In 1974, the Municipal Administration decided to celebrate the 350th anniversary of the discovery of St Rosalia's bones with the reconstruction of the Chariot. The idea of a modern interpretation was rejected, and the Chariot was rebuilt in forms inspired by those of the 18C models, thus emphasizing the determination to restore Palermo's great tradition of "festival machines".

Another important tradition is the *acchianata* (ascent) to Mount Pellegrino, i.e. the pil-

Festino of St Rosalia. A stall selling the characteristic "calia e simenza" (dried chickpeas and seeds).

Festino of St Rosalia. " Flying Angels" at Porta Felice.

Festino of St Rosalia. "Firework display" in the Marina promenade.

Festino of St Rosalia. The statue of the Santuzza on the Triumphal Chariot.

grimage on foot along the ancient path to the cave of the *Santuzza* (as Palermitans affectionately call their patron saint), which takes place on 4 September, the day of St Rosalia's death. On 6-8 September another famous pilgrimage is made to the Sanctuary of the Madonna della Milicia, at Altavilla Milicia.

From the 15C onwards, Greek and Albanian communities moved to Sicily, fleeing from their countries of origin after the Ottoman invasion. These have maintained all their original traditions, incorporating them into Sicilian folklore. At Piana degli Albanesi, Mezzojuso, Contessa Entellina, Palazzo Adriano and Santa Cristina Gela, festivities such as Christmas, the Epiphany and particularly Easter are still celebrated in accordance with the most authentic Byzantine rite. On these occasions, the women wear beautiful and precious antique costumes. Byzantine rites are also celebrated in Palermo, in the ancient Church of Santa Maria dell'Ammiraglio (the "Martorana"), now San Nicola di Mira, which is the sister Cathedral of the Eparchy of Piana degli Albanesi.

Mondello

Some 10 km from Palermo, and linked to the city by frequent bus services, Mondello is one of the most elegant and best-equipped bathing resorts in Sicily. It lies in a splendid position on the bay between Capo Gallo and the slopes of Mount Pellegrino, to the north-west of the city. Its beach (about 1.5 km long) is the favourite holiday destination not only of Palermitans, but also of a large number of tourists who have appreciated the efficiency of its facilities, the beautiful scenery and the luxuriant Mediterranean vegetation which makes Mondello a garden city. In addition to its bathing establishments, the resort offers a wide range of recreation facilities as well as opportunities for relaxing. There is a small tourist port for pleasure boats, and fishing and waterskiing can be practised offshore. Mondello offers excellent accommodation facilities, ranging from de-luxe to medium-level hotels, restaurants, open-air cinemas, discos and numerous bars. Palermitan gourmets are fond of the famous "polipari" who have their stands in the village square. Here you can taste the renowned freshly-boiled octopus ("polipo") sprinkled with lemon juice, as well as shellfish such as mussels and sea urchins. Before being transformed into the present-day elegant and picturesque bathing resort, Mondello was an ancient fortified tunny-fishery (the "Watchtower" can still be seen near the village square) at the edges of a swampy region infested with malaria. The territory of Valdesi was formerly used as a salt pan. Later, at the end of the 18C, part of this area was incorporated into the Favorita Royal Park created by King Ferdinand of Bourbon during his stay in Palermo. Between the 19C and 20C, with the construction of a main sewer with two outlets to the sea, the area was reclaimed and its tourist development promoted. It was franchised to an Italo-Belgian company which provided it with suitable bathing facilities, including the characteristic, large bathing establishment on a pier of concrete piles, which was built in 1912 and is still open to the public.

Mondello.
Panoramic view from Mount Pellegrino.

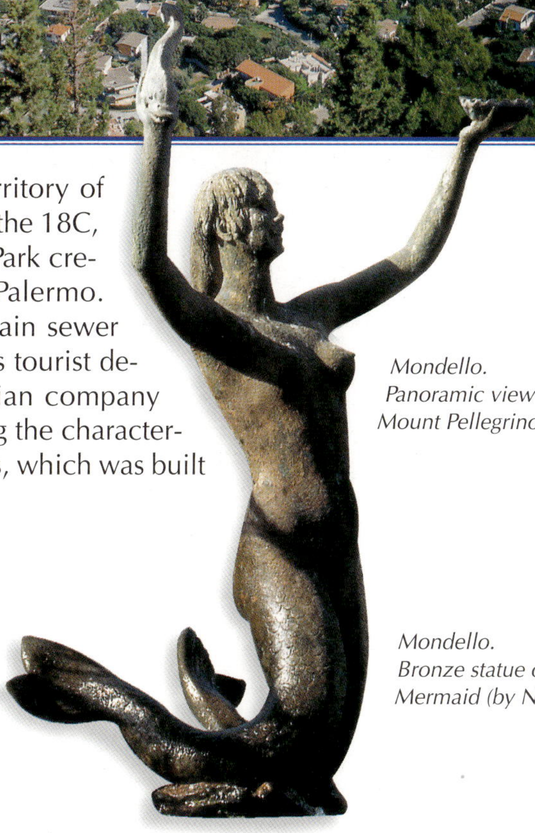

Mondello.
Bronze statue of the Mermaid (by N. Geraci).

Mount Pellegrino, Sanctuary of St Rosalia. Exterior.

Sanctuary of St Rosalia. The statue of the sleeping Santuzza.

Mount Pellegrino

This high promontory (*mons peregrinus* = solitary mountain), which bounds the gulf of Palermo to the north-west, is a calcareous massif with fairly steep slopes, which has recently been replanted with pines, false acacias and eucalyptus trees. The Addaura caves, on its north flank, are of considerable archaeological interest. Substantial evidence of human settlements dating from the Upper Paleolithic has been found there (engravings and pottery). The so-called "Addaura 2" cave, in particular, contains engravings which depict animal and human figures, perhaps celebrating a religious rite. Similar engravings – depicting only animal figures – are to be found in the Niscemi cave, on the east slope of the mountain looking onto the Favorita Park. Other caves have yielded numerous archaeological finds from later ages. The Addaura area (from the Latin *Ad Lauram*) owes its name to the local lauras (caves transformed into dwelling places) inhabited by monks in various historical periods, both before and after the year 1000. In the 12C, Rosalia Sini-

Sanctuary of St Rosalia. Interior of the cave.

baldi followed the example of these communities of hermits and retired to one of these caves, where groups of Basilian nuns also lived. In 1624, while a plague epidemic was raging across Palermo, the bones of the virgin Rosalia Sinibaldi were found in one of these caves, embedded in the calcareous alabaster which abounds in the area. The bones were carried in procession through the city and, according to the chronicles of the time, the plague ended. In 1625, a sanctuary in honour of the virgin (who was proclaimed patron saint of the city) was built on the site where her remains had been discovered. The sanctuary, which has since then attracted crowds of pilgrims, can be reached by the panoramic road winding up the mountain or on foot, along the pilgrims' ancient cobbled path. Pilgrimages along this path still take place annually, on 4 September (St Rosalia's *dies natalis*). A large flight of steps leads up to the 17C sanctuary (624 m above sea level). A vestibule and an entrance hall with a host of *ex-votos* lead into the cave where, according to tradition, the Saint lived her hermit's life. This is about 25 m deep; the water oozing from its walls is believed to have miraculous powers. On the left, under a canopy, is the statue of St Rosalia, covered in gold leaf. It is the work of Gregorio Tedeschi and was donated by King Charles of Bourbon. Adjoining the vestibule is a small museum housing sacred objects, gifts and *ex-votos*. Two roads start from the square, one leading to a hillock with a sheer cliff falling down to the sea, where there is a statue of the Saint, the other winding its way down to Mondello.

Monreale and *Castellaccio* of Monreale

Monreale is reached from Piazza Indipendenza (Palermo) by way of Corso Calatafimi and a panoramic road decorated with picturesque fountains. The final section of this road, which was created in the 18C, climbs steeply and, after two sharp bends and a straight stretch, leads to the small town on the slopes of Mount Caputo, mainly famous for its Duomo, which is one of the masterpieces of western medieval architecture.

Why did William II build this huge architectural complex not far from Palermo, where a Cathedral already existed, and why was the construction financed by the monarch? The reason is that the Hautevilles, who founded the *Regnum Siciliae*, were "apostolic legates" of the Popes in Rome and could create new bishoprics and "appoint" bishops who were later confirmed by the Popes. In order to somehow account for their great expenditure in the building of the two Cathedrals (at Monreale and in Palermo), King William II and the Bishop of Palermo, Gualtiero, were compelled to circulate legends on the miraculous discovery of enormous treasures under divine guidance. The simultaneous construction of the two majestic cathedrals – which indeed led to an architectural competition – reflected the struggle for political supremacy between the Crown and Palermo's Diocesan Curia or, rather, between the Kingdom of Sicily and the Pope in Rome. The Hauteville sovereigns, as vassals of the Pope and

Opposite page: Monreale, Piazza Vittorio Emanuele. The fountain of Triton (by M. Rutelli). In the background, the Duomo.
Large photo: Monreale. Panoramic view of the town and of the Conca d'Oro plain from the lower slopes of Mount Caputo.

Duomo of Monreale. West front with the two towers.
Bottom: Capital in the interior of the Duomo.

Next page: Duomo of Monreale. The nave and, at the far end, the transept and central apse.

papal legates, "appointed" all the Latin bishops of the island, choosing them from the most loyal of their men.

However, when it came to the Bishop of Palermo, the question was not so easy. In 1072, on their arrival in the city which had just been liberated from the Saracens, the Hauteville brothers were surprised to find a Bishop, Nicodemus. Like all his predecessors during the Saracen rule, he had lived isolated in the small Church of Santa Ciriaca, in the present-day Monreale, where the Duomo was to be built. The historical continuity of the Palermitan diocese had thus been ensured during the long Saracen occupation. Therefore, the appointment of the Bishop of Palermo was not a prerogative of the kings of Sicily but of the Canons of the Cathedral, who were subjected solely to the Pope. This gave the Bishop of Palermo special autonomy and authority vis-à-vis the Crown. Gualtiero was appointed Bishop of the city in 1168. From the very beginning, the policy he adopted was intended to be as autonomous as possible from the Crown's directives. He had just taken office, in 1169, when an earthquake irreparably damaged the old Cathedral. In 1170 he began to demolish the unsafe parts of the building and to reconstruct it in more majestic architectural forms.

Hence, King William had no time to waste. In 1174, while Gualtiero was demolishing the old Cathedral, he had already begun to build his Duomo at Monreale, together with a large Abbey and a royal residence. He created a new Bishopric and extended its jurisdiction over such a vast territory that the Bishopric of Palermo was almost "caught up" within it.

ARCHANGEL MI CHAEL.
ARCHAN GELUS.

Duomo of Monreale. Byzantine mosaics (12C). Top: Christ Pantocrator (the Lord of the Universe).

Opposite page: The Creation of the Sea and Earth. Bottom: The Creation of Fish and Birds.

The privilege of housing the royal tombs was also transferred to the Duomo of Monreale. Both cathedrals were left incomplete, albeit with many differences. The competition between the monarchs and the Primate of Sicily reflected a political conflict typical of the western Middle Ages. Another example is the long contest between Henry II Plantagenet, king of England, and the Primate of England, Thomas Becket, Archbishop of Canterbury. Indeed, a few years after his murder on the steps of the high altar of his cathedral, Becket was depicted in a mosaic in the main apse of the Duomo of Monreale.

In 1172, having come of age and ascended to the throne, King William II began to build the monumental complex of Monreale. Work was carried out so rapidly that, by 1185, the main architectural structures had been completed. As early as August

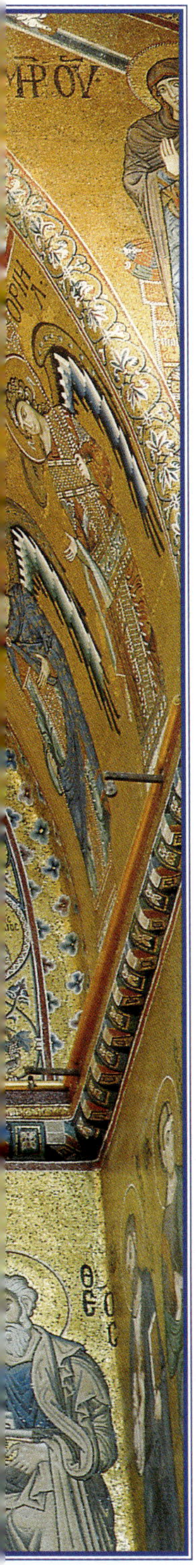

1176, William dedicated the new church to Our Lady of the Assumption (which means that at least the Sanctuary had been completed) and granted great privileges and vast estates to the Benedictine monks from Cava dei Tirreni (in Campania) who had been summoned to settle in the new monastery at Monreale. Only in 1183 did Pope Lucius III raise Monreale to a Bishop's See (*"Licit Dominus"* bull). In 1185, the magnificent bronze door by Bonanno da Pisa was mounted in the main entrance. When William died, in 1189, his dream had been fulfilled. The construction of the Monastery, which probably began simultaneously with that of the Duomo, was completed with the creation of the Cloister (1176-1189). Of the other structures, only the walls of the south wing (perhaps the dormitory) have remained intact. It may be assumed that the building was either extended or restructured after the reign of William II. This assumption also holds for the Royal Palace. The discovery of a number of architectural elements seems to indicate that it was incorporated into structures built later than the 12C and partly used as the Town Hall. However, recent finds made on the west side of the square, where the main entrance to the Duomo is, have suggested that the building might have been located on a different site. The date of construction of at least three fronts of the boundary walls of the complex is still controversial. Most of the existing stretches seem to date from later than the 12C.

The design of the Duomo of Monreale is typical of the great religious architecture promoted by the Hauteville kings of Sicily in the 12C. This was based on the combination of a majestic two-aisle building of Cassinese inspiration (Benedictine architecture of the Montecassino Monastery) with a part of the central-plan Byzantine church typical of this period (a Greek cross with arms of equal length). The three apses, which protrude considerably, face east. The most important part of the Duomo, in fact, is its east front with the three monumental apses, which projected outwards the liturgical significance of the Sanctuary. To understand the full importance of this front – a true architectural jewel in its own right – it should also be considered that it was the one most conspicuous

from the road which, crossing the Royal Park, led from Palermo to Monreale. Due to the changed surroundings, however, it takes a considerable effort of imagination to "recreate" this view.

Top, left:
The temptation of Adam and Eve.

Top, right:
Madonna Odigitria.

Bottom:
The Last Supper.

Top, left: Willian II dressed as a Byzantine "Basileus", presenting a model of the Duomo to the Virgin Mary.

Top, right: William II crowned by Christ in accordance with the official Byzantine iconography.

The decoration of the apsidal walls is complex and impressive. It is centred around plastic and elegant relief elements: small columns in the two upper orders rest on slender piers and support two series of intertwined blind arches which embellish the protruding walls, creating a refined architectural effect. The blind ogival arches are enhanced by frames and enclose different levels of decorative bands and discs characterized by limestone and lava polychrome inlays, whereas the walls are plastered. The play of colours created by the stone inlays is reminiscent of that observed in the monuments of Amalfi and Ravello, another region of the Kingdom which was strongly influenced by Byzantine decorative forms. This type of external decoration was to prove very successful. It was reproduced in other churches, including the apses of Palermo Cathedral, which, however, lack the richness and complexity of their counterparts in Monreale.

The main front is characterized by two rustic corner towers flanking the great portal. A narthex was presumably built between the two towers in the 12C, and was later dismantled. The present-day portico, with three great arches in classicizing forms, was built in 1770 and contrasts sharply with the medieval aspect of the front. The two towers were a recurrent motif in the great Sicilian cathedrals financed by the Crown. An example of this is the Duomo of Cefalù, where these elements of the front have remained intact. The entrance to the Duomo of Monreale is embellished by a magnificent marble portal and bronze door, an ensemble known as the "Gate to Paradise". Its architectural frame features Hellenistic motifs such as plant volutes with intertwined human and animal figures. The two-leafed bronze door by Bonanno da Pisa

(1186) is decorated with 46 panels depicting episodes of the Old and New Testaments. The four lower panels represent pairs of lions and griffins. The other two-leafed bronze door, by Barisano da Trani, is surrounded by a rectangular stone frame with geometric motifs. It is decorated with 28 panels depicting battle scenes, stories of saints, oriental-inspired heraldic animals, plant and floral motifs.

The nave and aisles are divided by 18 tall columns, 9 on each side, resting on tall bases and crowned by Corinthian and figured capitals. The latter depict the faces of

Duomo of Monreale. The three apses facing east.

Ceres and Juno within medallions framed by cornucopias. Tall dosserets bear pointed arches; above are the windows which, externally, alternate with blind windows, all of which are framed by stone inlaid decorations. The internal walls of the church are entirely covered with glittering Byzantine mosaics, with the only exception of a broad marble wainscot. In the right wing of the Sanctuary are the tombs of William I and William II. In the left wing are those of Margaret of Navarre (the wife of William I and mother of William II), her sons Roger and Henry, and Louis IX, king of France.

The mosaics cover a total surface area of over 6,000 sq m. They were completed in a few years (probably between 1180 and 1190) by skilful mosaicists who coordinated their work with that of the other craftsmen. All the episodes – some more expressive, others more realistic and descriptive, or more concise and simpler – are characterized by a deep sense of poetic unity. The figurative ensemble is coherent from both the aesthetic-decorative and the dogmatic-theological points of view, the latter

aspect also being fundamental to the arrangement of themes and figures in accordance with the Byzantine tradition. The theme of the "Word made flesh" is developed in three well-defined cycles: the expectation of the coming of Christ and episodes from the Old Testament; the coming of Christ; the continuation of His mission by the Church. A host of episodes and an endless crowd of characters from all times entirely cover the high walls of the Temple. The ensemble is dominated by the majestic and severe figure of Christ Pantocrator (the Lord of the Universe) in the bowl-shaped vault of the central apse.

A description of these mosaics – however concise – would require a specialized guide on the subject. For brevity's sake, only two particularly interesting panels of the Sanctuary will be described here. The first, above the royal throne, depicts King William wearing ceremonial clothes and receiving the royal crown from Christ, in accordance with an iconographic model which was a prerogative of the Roman emperors of Constantinople. In the second panel, above the Archbishop's cathedra, William (here again

Duomo of Monreale.
West entrance portal with the two-leafed bronze door by Bonanno Pisano (1186).

Duomo of Monreale.
The Chapel of the Crucifix, a magnificent example of "variegated marble" decoration.

dressed as a Byzantine Basileus) is kneeling before the Madonna, presenting her a model of the Duomo. The thousands of figures and episodes were intended to serve a didactic purpose, providing religious teaching to the population of the district of Monreale. This resulted in the greatest and most articulated iconographic project ever conceived and accomplished for religious didactic purposes in the 12C. It can be considered as a majestic work in the field of international mosaic production, and as the greatest masterpiece of its kind ever produced in the western world. Although

The Cloister. Capital depicting William II in the act of presenting a model of the Duomo to the Virgin Mary.

the "hand" of different authors is evident, the mosaics are characterized by a uniform style.

The cloister of the Monastery is the best-preserved example of this type of 12C construction in Sicily and, at the same time, the largest and most beautiful of those which have come down to us. It is square in plan, with 208 small paired columns resting on a low parapet. On the north-west corner of the cloister there is a small roofless portico, square in plan, with three arches on each of the two sides jutting out into the garden and a fountain of great formal elegance. A slender column set in the centre of the basin bears a spherical bulb from which water gushes out. The capitals of the cloister are the work of various sculptors, as is witnessed by their heterogeneous forms which, however, enrich the overall effect. Scholars have given conventional names to these otherwise unknown artists. The so-called "Master of the Dedication" can be recognized by his very small but somewhat elegant figures. He is the author of the famous capital which depicts King William wearing the *Kamelaukion* crown, typical of Byzantine emperors, in the act of presenting a model of the Duomo to the Virgin Mary. Another sculptor, named "the Master of the

Mission of the Apostles", privileges a more substantial plastic representation of the figures. The "Master of Putti" is easily recognized by the figures of young boys present in his works, also in the form of telamones. The "Master of Eagles" shows a preference for birds. The only signature is that of a marble-worker, who handed its name down to posterity as "*Filius Costantinus Marmorarius*".

Those who do not mind taking a steep walk and love fine natural scenery should not miss a visit to the Castellaccio, a medieval castle on the summit of Mount Caputo

The Cloister. Overall view. A refined blend of architecture, sculpture and decorative arts, the Cloister was the work of craftsmen from all the territories ruled by the Kingdom of Sicily in the 12C.

The Cloister.
The small angular patio ("chiostrino", or little cloister) with a fountain.

Decorative details of the columns at the corners of the "chiostrino".

Bundle of four columns
in the "chiostrino".

(766 m above sea level), not far from Monreale. A narrow track (about 3 km long) leads to this interesting 12C building which has the quadrangular plan typical of the late-Byzantine castra. At the end of the 14C, Manfredi Chiaramonte had the merlons and rounds of the castle demolished in order to prevent its use by his enemies. The exterior has seven curtain towers. The ancient boundary walls and the three apses of a large chapel used by the monks of Monreale have been preserved. The building was completely restored by G. Patricolo in 1898. The site offers a vast panorama of the surrounding area. In the past, in fact, the castle provided an elevated observation point over the Conca d'Oro, Monreale, the Royal Park and Palermo.

San Martino delle Scale. View of the Benedictine Monastery from above.

San Martino delle Scale

San Martino delle Scale, a holiday and health resort (500-600 m above sea level) surrounded by a recently planted wood, can be reached by the road which, starting from Boccadifalco, crosses the Valle del Paradiso between Mount Cuccio and Mount Caputo. The Benedictine Abbey, originally built by Pope Gregory the Great in the 6C, is very interesting. The complex was destroyed by the Muslims in the 9C and rebuilt in 1347 on the initiative of Emanuele Spinola, the Archbishop of nearby Monreale. Of the 14C construction, only part of a south-west loggia remains today. The church and the earliest nucleus of the present-day monastery date from the 16C, but the complex was enlarged and enriched in the following centuries. In particular, the east wing was built in the 18C to a project by the architect Venanzio Marvuglia. Inside the Abbey is a sumptuous vestibule with 16 Billiemi stone columns. Below the pincer-shaped staircase is the sculptural group of "St Martin offering his mantle to the Beggar", by Ignazio Marabitti. The frescoed ceiling of the refectory, depicting "Daniel in the Lions' Den", is the work of Pietro Novelli. At the foot of the bell tower is the Oreto Fountain, another work by Ignazio Marabitti. The church also contains valuable works of art, including numerous paintings by Giuseppe Salerno, known as "lo Zoppo di Ganci", and by the Neapolitan painter Paolo De Matteis. There are also two paintings by Pietro Novelli: "St Benedict handing his sword to Sancho III of Castile", above the altar in the transept wing, and a "Madonna between St Benedict and St Scolastica" on the 15C portal near the transept. Above the walnut choir, carved in 1591 by Benvenuto Tortelli of Brescia and Campanian craftsmen, is an organ by Raffaele La Valle.

San Martino delle Scale. Triumphal sculptural ensemble at the top of the fine fountain by Ignazio Marabitti (1782), with the personification of the Oreto river.

PALERMO

MUSEUMS AND ART GALLERIES
Modern Art Gallery "Empedocle Restivo"
Via Filippo Turati, 10 – Tel. 091 588 951
Sicilian Regional Gallery "Palazzo Abatellis"
Via Alloro, 4 – Tel. 0916 230 011
Regional Archaeological Museum "Antonio Salinas" Piazza Olivella – Tel. 0916 116 806
Diocesan Museum
Via Matteo Bonello, 2 – Tel. 0916 077 111
Mormino Foundation Museum
Viale della Libertà, 52 – Tel. 0916 080 111
Geological Museum "G. Gemmellaro"
Corso Tuköry, 131 – Tel. 0917 041 051
International Museum of Puppetry
Via Butera, 1 – Tel. 091 328 060
Sicilian Ethnographic Museum "Giuseppe Pitrè"
Via Duca degli Abruzzi - Tel. 0917 404 890
Palazzo Mirto Museum
Via Merlo, 2 - Tel. 0916 164 751
Museum of the Risorgimento
Piazza S. Domenico, 1 – Tel. 091 582 774

CHURCHES AND ORATORIES
Palatine Chapel (San Pietro)
Piazza Parlamento, 1 - Tel. 0917 051 111
Cathedral (Maria Santissima Assunta)
Corso Vittorio Emanuele - Tel. 091 334 376
Church of Gesù (Casa Professa)
Piazza Casa Professa, 21 - Tel. 0916 076 111
Church of the Santissimo Salvatore
Corso V. Emanuele, 395 - Tel. 091 323 392
Church of the Madonna della Pietà
Via Torremuzza - Tel. 0916 165 266
Church of the Santissima Trinità (Magione)
Piazza Magione, 44 – Tel. 0916 170 596
Church of Sant'Anna
Piazza Sant'Anna - Tel. 0916 171 225
Church of Sant'Agostino
Via Sant'Agostino - Tel. 091 584 632
Church of San Cataldo
Piazza Bellini, 3
Church of Santa Cita
Via Squarcialupo - Tel. 091 332 779
Church of San Domenico
Piazza San Domenico - Tel. 091 584 872
Church of San Francesco d'Assisi
Piazza San F.sco d'Assisi - Tel. 0916 162 819
Church of San Francesco Saverio
Piazza San F.sco Saverio - Tel. 0916 517 052
Church of San Giorgio dei Genovesi
Piazza San Giorgio dei Genovesi
Church of San Giovanni degli Eremiti
Via dei Benedettini, 18 - Tel. 0916 515 019
Church of San Giovanni dei Lebbrosi
Via S. Cappello, 38 – Tel. 091 475 024
Church of San Giuseppe dei Teatini
Corso Vittorio Emanuele - Tel. 091 331 239
Church of Sant'Ignazio all'Olivella
Piazza Olivella, 9 - Tel. 091 586 867
Church of Santa Maria dell'Ammiraglio (Martorana)
Piazza Bellini, 3 - Tel. 0916 161 692
Church of Santa Maria degli Angeli (Gancia)
Via Alloro, 27 - Tel. 0916 165 221
Church of Santa Maria della Catena
Piazza delle Dogane - Tel. 0916 067 111
Church of Santa Maria dei Miracoli
Piazza Marina
Church of Santa Maria di Valverde
Largo Cavalieri di Malta
Church of the "Spasimo"
Via dello Spasimo - Tel. 0916 161 486
Church of San Matteo Apostolo
Corso Vittorio Emanuele, 257 - Tel. 091 334 833
Church of Santa Teresa alla Kalsa
Piazza Kalsa - Tel. 0916 171 658
Church of Santo Spirito (del Vespro)
Sant'Orsola Cemetery - Tel. 091 422 691
Oratory of the Rosario
Via dei Bambinai
Oratory of San Lorenzo
Via dell'Immacolatella
Sanctuary of Santa Rosalia
Mount Pellegrino - Tel. 091 540 326

MONUMENTS AND PALACES
Castellammare
Via Patti
Capuchin Catacombs
Piazza Cappuccini, 1 - Tel. 091 212 633
Cuba
Corso Calatafimi, 100
Cubula
Corso Calatafimi (Villa Napoli)
Fontana del Garraffo
Corso Vittorio Emanuele/Piazza Marina
Fontana Pretoria ("delle vergogne")
Piazza Pretoria
Palazzo Aiutamicristo
Via Garibaldi
Archbishop's Palace
Via Matteo Bonello, 2
Palazzo Chiaramonte
Piazza Marina, 60
Palazzo Ganci-Valguarnera
Piazza Sant'Anna
Royal Palace (Palazzo dei Normanni)
Piazza Parlamento, 1 - Tel. 0917 051 111
Palazzo Sclafani
Piazzetta S. Giovanni Decollato
Villa Igiea
Via Belmonte, 43
Villino Basile
Via Siracusa, 15
Villino Florio
Viale Regina Margherita
Zisa
Piazza Guglielmo il Buono - Tel. 0916 520 269

ARCHIVES AND LIBRARIES
State Archives
Corso V. Emanuele, 3 - Tel. 0917 406 010
Municipal Archives
Via Maqueda, 157 - 0916 172 625
Sicilian Regional Library
Corso V. Emanuele, 431 - Tel. 0916 967 642
Municipal Library
Piazza Casa Professa - Tel. 0917 602 362
Franciscan Library
Piazza San F.sco d'Assisi – Tel. 0916 162 819

THEATRES
Teatro Biondo
Via Roma, 258 - Tel. 091 582 364
Teatro Massimo
Piazza Verdi - Tel. 0916 053 111
Teatro Politeama Garibaldi
Via Turati, 2

PARKS AND GARDENS
Giardino Garibaldi
Piazza Marina
Giardino Inglese
Viale della Libertà - Tel. 0917 405 756
Botanical Garden
Via A. Lincoln, 2b – Tel. 0916 238 111
La Favorita Park
Piazza Leoni - Piazza Gen.le Cascino
Villa d'Orleans Park
Corso Re Ruggero
Villa Bonanno
Piazza della Vittoria
Villa Giulia
Via A. Lincoln - Tel. 0917 404 028
Villa Niscemi
Piazza dei Quartieri
Villa Trabia
Via A. Salinas, 3 - Tel. 0917 405 905

MONREALE

Duomo
Piazza Duomo - Tel. 0916 404 413
Benedictine Cloister
Piazza Guglielmo il Buono - Tel. 0916 404 403
Information Centre
Piazza V. Emanuele - Tel. 0916 466 070

SAN MARTINO DELLE SCALE
Organized tours - Tel. 091 418 104 - 418 195

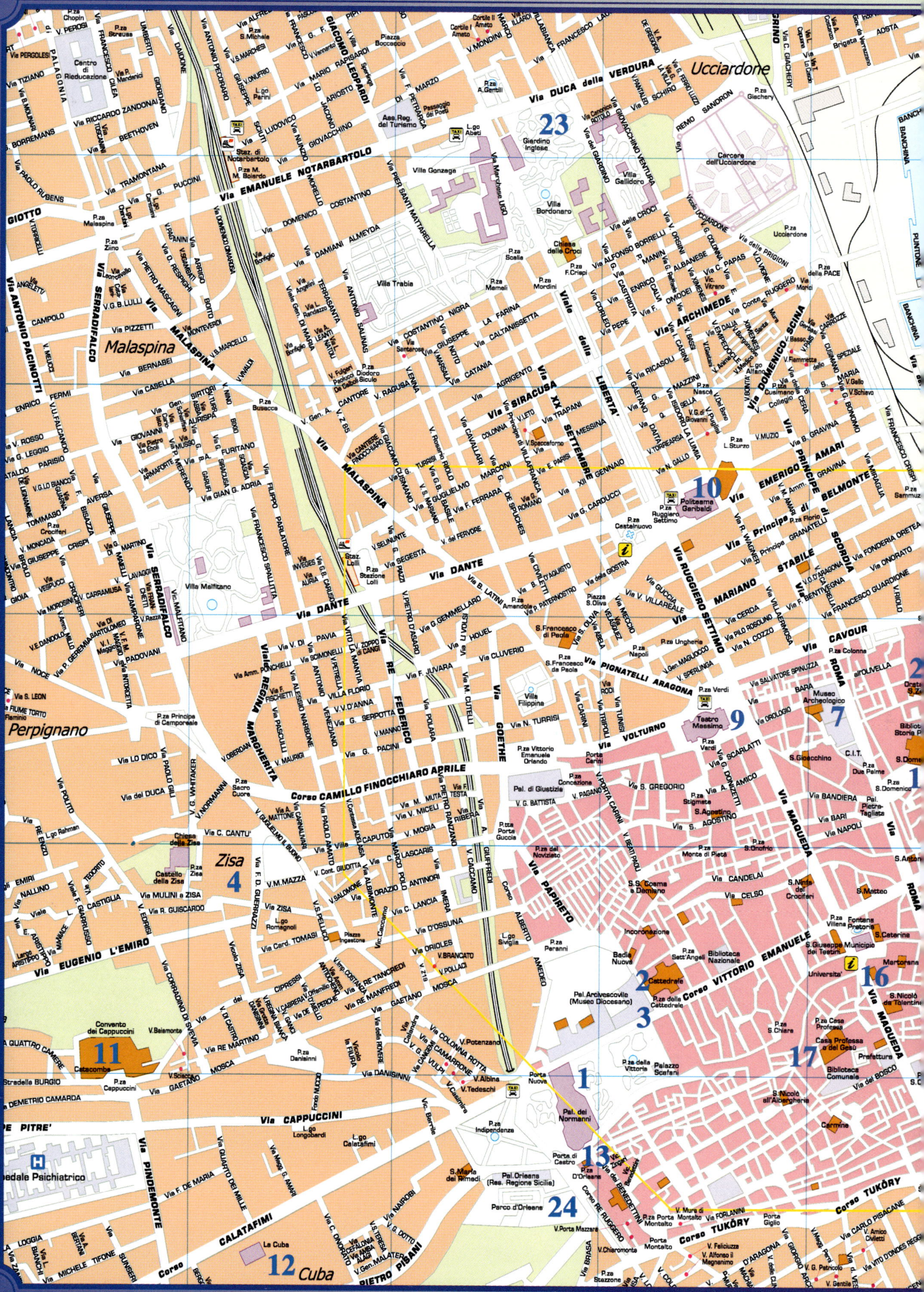
Ucciardone
Carcere dell'Ucciardone
Via DUCA della VERDURA
Giardino Inglese
23
Villa Gonzaga
Villa Trabia
Villa Bordonaro
Villa Gallidoro
Chiesa delle Croci
Via EMANUELE NOTARBARTOLO
Via MARCHESE UGO
Via SIRACUSA
Viale della LIBERTA'
Via XX SETTEMBRE
Via ARCHIMEDE
Via DOMENICO SCINA
Via PRINCIPE di BELMONTE
Via EMERIGO AMARI
Politeama Garibaldi
10
Via RUGGIERO SETTIMO
Via MARIANO STABILE
Via CAVOUR
Via ROMA
Museo Archeologico
7
Teatro Massimo
9
Via MAQUEDA
Malaspina
Via MALASPINA
Via SERRADIFALCO
Via ANTONIO PACINOTTI
Villa Malfitano
Via DANTE
Via RE FEDERICO
Via GOETHE
Villa Filippina
Via PIGNATELLI ARAGONA
Via VOLTURNO
Perpignano
Viale REGINA MARGHERITA
Corso CAMILLO FINOCCHIARO APRILE
Pal. di Giustizia
Via PAPIRETO
Zisa
4
Castello della Zisa
Chiesa della Zisa
Via EUGENIO L'EMIRO
Convento dei Cappuccini
11
Catacombe
Via CAPPUCCINI
Via PINDEMONTE
Ospedale Psichiatrico
Corso CALATAFIMI
La Cuba
12 Cuba
Cattedrale
2
Pal. Arcivescovile (Museo Diocesano)
3
Corso VITTORIO EMANUELE
Porta Nuova
1
Pal. dei Normanni
P.za Indipendenza
Pal. Orleans (Res. Regione Sicilia)
Parco d'Orleans
24
13
Corso TUKÒRY
Biblioteca Nazionale
Casa Professa o del Gesù
17
16
Martorana
Via del BOSCO

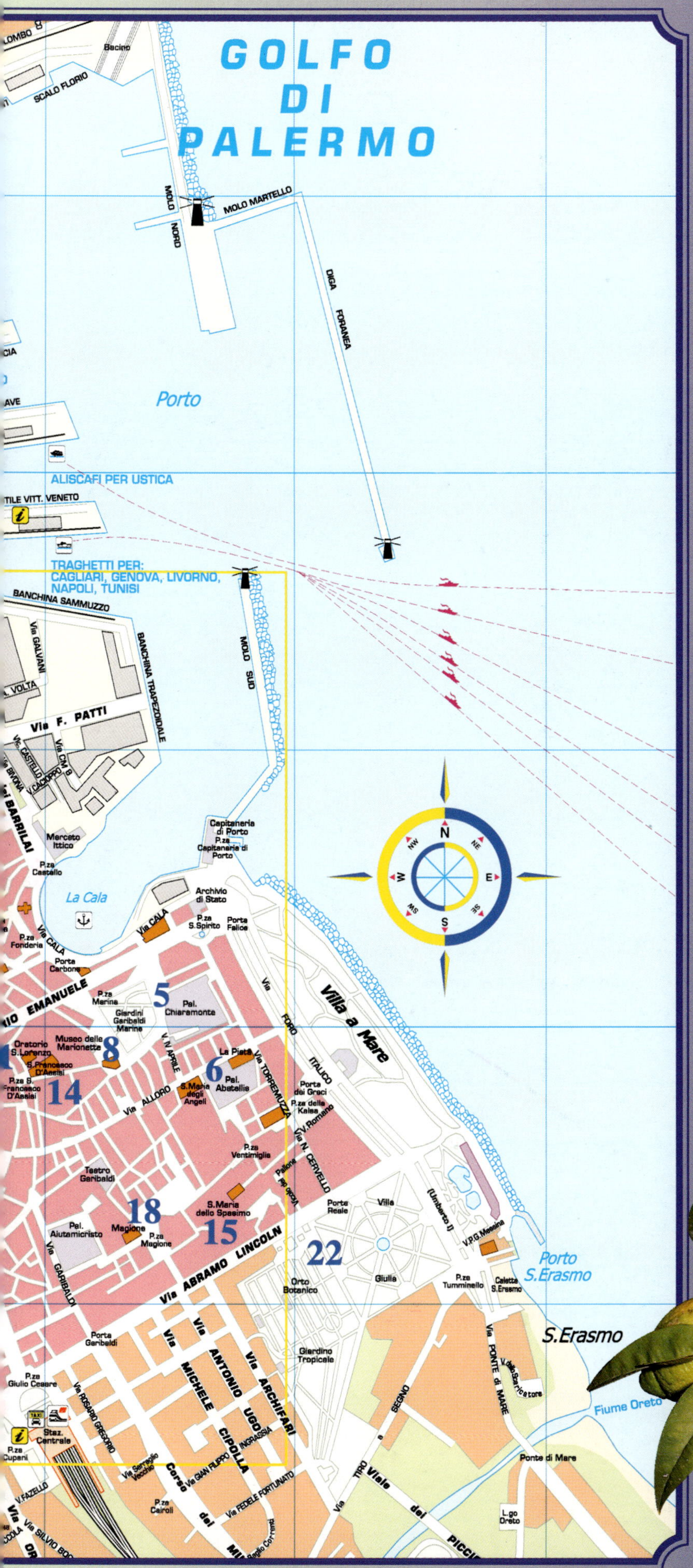

LEGEND

1 - Royal Palace (Palazzo dei Normanni)
Palatine Chapel (San Pietro)
2 - Cathedral
3 - Archbishop's Palace
Diocesan Museum
4 - Zisa
5 - Palazzo Chiaramonte (Steri)
6 - Sicilian Regional Gallery
7 - Regional Archaeological Museum
8 - International Museum of Puppetry
9 - Teatro Massimo
10 - Teatro Politeama "Garibaldi"
11 - Capuchin Catacombs
12 - Cuba
13 - Church of San Giovanni degli Eremiti
14 - Church of San Francesco d'Assisi
15 - Church of the "Spasimo"
16 - Church of Santa Maria dell'Ammiraglio (Martorana)
17 - Church of Gesù (Casa Professa)
18 - Church of the SS. Trinità (Magione)
19 - Church of San Domenico
Museum of the Risorgimento
20 - Oratory of the Rosario
(Church of Santa Cita)
21 - Oratory of San Lorenzo
22 - Botanical Garden - Villa Giulia
23 - Giardino Inglese
24 - Villa d'Orleans Park

Contents

Printed by Officine Grafiche Riunite - Palermo
January 2004